FREDERICK DOUGLASS

Frederick Douglass

A Precursor of Liberation Theology

To: DR. Steve Melamed

Thank you for your support and friendship—Yours in the struggle

Reginald F. Davis

Reginald F. Davis

Mercer University Press
Macon, Georgia
25th Anniversary

iv

ISBN 0-86554-925-7
MUP/P312

© 2005 Mercer University Press
1400 Coleman Avenue
Macon, Georgia 31207
All rights reserved

First Edition.

The paper used in this publication meets the minimum requirements of
American National Standard for Information Sciences—Permanence of
Paper for Printed Library Materials, ANSI Z39.48-1992.

Library of Congress Cataloging-in-Publication Data

Davis, Reginald F., 1964-
Frederick Douglass : a precursor of liberation theology / Reginald F.
Davis.— 1st ed.
v. cm.
Includes bibliographical references and index.
Contents: Evolution to a liberation theology—Douglass : an eloquent voice
against oppression—Douglass attacks the maintenance needs of oppression :
racism, sexism, beliefs, and values—Douglass and the making of a liberation
theology—Interpretation of Douglass as a liberation thinker.
ISBN 0-86554-925-7 (pbk. : alk. paper)
1. Douglass, Frederick, 1818-1895—Political and social views. 2. Douglass,
Frederick, 1818-1895—Religion. 3. Douglass, Frederick, 1818-
1895—Philosophy. 4. Liberation theology. 5. Christianity and
politics—United States. I. Title.
E449.D75D385 2005
973.8'092—dc22

2005002527

CONTENTS

PREFACE

All efforts I had previously made to secure my freedom,
had not only failed, but had seemed only to rivet my fetters the
more firmly and to render my escape more difficult. Baffled,
entangled and discouraged, I had at times asked myself the
question, may not my condition after all be God's work and
ordered for a wise purpose, and if so, was not submission my
duty? A contest had in fact been going on in my mind for a long
time, between the clear consciousness of right and the plausible
make shift of theology and superstition. The one held me an
abject slave—a prisoner for life, punished for some
transgression in which I had no lot or part; the other counseled
me to manly endeavor to secure my freedom. This contest was
ended; my chains were broken, and the victory brought me
unspeakable joy.[1]

There is no gainsaying that Frederick Douglass was one of the
most conspicuous advocates of human rights in the nineteenth
century. He rose from obscurity as a slave to an awesome
career as an eloquent national and international abolitionist

---

[1] Frederick Douglass, *The Life and Times of Frederick Douglass* (New
York: Pathway, 1941) 225.

viii

lecturer, a newspaper editor, a successful author, a recruiter for the Union army, a statesman, and a women's rights advocate. Douglass stood uncowed against oppression and the violation of human rights. He was an uncompromising man for the "immediate, unconditional, and universal" enfranchisement of those who were enslaved for centuries against their will. He cogently pointed out the practices of America and how they were inconsistent with the nation's religious and democratic creed. His biting jeremiads were directed not only toward the political platforms that kept the machinery of oppression operating, but also the hypocrisy of the church that was complicit in maintaining it.

It is my contention that Douglass anticipated a liberation theology, a theology that is at the heart of the Christian tradition to eradicate economic, social, and political oppression. Douglass was carving an emancipatory pedagogy out of the stone of oppression that weighed heavily upon him and his people. He knew that the religious practices of this land served one purpose only—to keep the oppressor on top and to make the oppressor more powerful. As long as the oppressor can convince the oppressed that their lot is designed and orchestrated by God, there will never be a balance of power between the groups. Therefore, Douglass spent a lifetime trying to correct the miseducation of the oppressed who had accepted their oppressors' religion and its interpretation, which meant relegating liberation to an eschatological orientation.

To help correct the miseducation of the oppressed, Douglass painstakingly deconstructed the theological and philosophical guardian religion that conserved and protected the walls of oppression. He knew that in order to bring about social reform, agitation was essential in acting to transform the social context in which the disinherited masses lived out their lives. The oppressed must be the ultimate evaluators of their situation. They must be the ones to label their situation and determine the kind of response needed to achieve their liberation. For example, Douglass pointed out that the same revolutionary spirit that brought about America's freedom and independence from the British was needed to bring about the liberation of the American slaves. Agitation is essential. The Founding Fathers demonstrated it to throw off the British yoke of oppression. Douglass stated that these were men of peace: "But they preferred revolution to peaceful submission to bondage. They were quiet men; but they did not shrink from agitating against oppression. They showed forbearance; but they knew its limits. They believed in order; but not in the order of tyranny. With them, nothing was 'settled' that was not right. With them justice, liberty and humanity were 'final' not slavery and oppression." Douglass believed the principles contained in the Declaration of Independence were good and moral principles and that America ought to be truthful to them "on all occasions, in all places, against all foes, and at whatever cost."[2]

In 1895, at the close of a brilliant career, a young man asked for Douglass's advice for a person just starting out. Douglass replied, "Agitate! Agitate! Agitate!"[3] Douglass understood that if the oppressed were to attain their liberation, it must be through the persistent agitation of the oppressor. But he knew that the antecedent to agitation is the need for a critical analysis to determine the nature of oppression. He understood that an enslaved people cannot move forward toward liberating themselves until they know who they are and who their oppressors are. Once this becomes clear, they must

[2] Frederick Douglass, "What to the Slave Is the Fourth of July?" Speech delivered in Corinthian Hall, Rochester, New York, 5 July 1852.
[3] Benjamin Quarles, ed. *Great Lives Observed.* (New Jersey: Prentice-Hall, Inc., 1968) 167.

act against those forces. This new awareness of selfhood would be the driving force behind the social agitation. The religious and political tradition would be reexamined to see if they worked at cross-purposes with liberation. For example, Douglass examined the religious tradition in America. Any religious beliefs and values that maintain oppression must be dumped, and those beliefs and values that facilitate liberation must be embraced. Douglass also examined the Constitution to determine its stance on slavery. If it was antislavery, then the enslaved would have to struggle to secure their rights within the Constitution.

The challenge here is to engage in the kind of education and agitation that would eliminate oppression. Douglass knew that the kind of education that would serve the struggle for liberation must be purged of the oppressors' consciousness, abstractness, and sterility. In order to gain autonomy and self-affirmation, the oppressed must first break from the psychological consciousness of the oppressor that has been deposited in them, which results in a kind of social quietism. Douglass's experience taught him that the kind of education the oppressed must embrace is the kind of education that is born out of struggle against oppression. It was out of this medium of education that Douglass discovered a new self. And this new self made his oppressors angry, bitter, and resentful of him. Yet largely because of his life as a reformer, the slaves were released from physical bondage; the Fourteenth and Fifteenth Amendments were passed, theoretically making African Americans equal before the law; the schools in Rochester, New York, were desegregated; and the Women's Rights movement was launched. Had Douglass been a victim of miseducation, he would not have been a powerful influence in changing the course of America.

As a vanguard for liberation, Douglass saw the great anomaly of a Christian-professing America that contradicted itself by its practice of oppression and paternalism. He saw that America was being destroyed not by any foreign power, but by the self-inflicted blows of holding others down in oppression from within and the religious justification that endorsed it. For example, America claims to be a land of freedom, celebrating the Fourth of July to show its independence, but the great contradiction was American slavery. Douglass knew that America could not "survive half slaves and half free." The contradiction would eventually reach a boiling point that would challenge the nation to chart another course or there would be no nation.

In an effort to help the nation chart another course, Douglass committed himself in the struggle for liberation with a two-fold purpose. His first purpose was to liberate the oppressed from their oppression, and the second purpose, not unlike the first, was to liberate the oppressors who did not have the moral capacity to liberate themselves. According to Paulo Freire, author of *Pedagogy of the Oppressed*, "The oppressors, who oppress, exploit, and rape by virtue of their power, cannot find in this power the strength to liberate either the oppressed or themselves. Only power that springs from the weakness of the oppressed will be sufficiently strong to free both."[4] Douglass lived and believed it was his calling, duty, and responsibility to assist with the salvation of both the oppressed and the oppressor. He was never content with his own salvation, and he believed it was his duty to help in the salvation of his people and those who oppressed them, and this should be the purpose and objective of any social reform.

---

[4] Paulo Freire, *Pedagogy of the Oppressed* (New York: Continuum Publishing Company, 1993) 26.

We label Douglass a liberation thinker not because he constructed a systemic theology, but because in his speeches, writings, and actions he hit upon parallel patterns of thought of liberation theology. Moreover, Douglass lived his theology. His life was a prime example of what the oppressed can do to gain and secure freedom. His theological position was the alternative for the oppressed who were seeking liberation in an oppressive society. Douglass's parallel patterns of thought of liberation theology were formed out of a context that he knew well, and he brought this to bear on this context so the context itself could be transformed by the gospel message of liberation.

ACKNOWLEDGMENTS

The writing of this book would not have been possible had it not been for my professors at Florida State University, especially William R. Jones, who believed I had something to contribute to the life and thought of Frederick Douglass. William R. Jones taught me the function and tilt of religion, and how religion can be used as an instrument to maintain the structures of oppression. While investigating the religious development of Douglass, it was clear that American Christianity tilted toward maintaining oppression, and Douglass spent a lifetime trying to correct it.

Not only did my professors at Florida State University think I had something to contribute to the study of Douglass, but professors at Garrett-Evangelical Theological Seminary, where I was Dean of Students, confirmed the contribution. I want to thank Rosemary Ruether for helping me to avoid being anachronistic in the pursuit to prove that Douglass was a precursor of liberation theology. Also, I would like to thank Mercer University Press for accepting this book for publication.

I cannot thank my God and my family enough for the many years of support and encouragement I have received since I embarked upon this journey. My family has supported my desire to complete this study. It was their encouragement, especially my wife Myrlene Davis, that helped me to press on until it was done. It is to them that I dedicate this work.

1

Evolution to a
Liberation Thinker

Frederick Douglass was one of the greatest personalities in the nineteenth century to address parallel patterns of thought in liberation theology. Notwithstanding, countless others helped cast the die for a theology of liberation. But since Douglass was the most conspicuous abolitionist, his speeches, writings, and lectures were the most widely known to those struggling against inhumanity. Douglass's contributions to human freedom and dignity have made him a shining prince in the history of America. Douglass prepared himself to challenge the idea that slavery was designed and orchestrated by God; defying slavery was his moral obligation.

Born in Tuckahoe, Maryland, in February 1817, Frederick Augustus Washington Bailey, later known as Frederick Douglass, was raised and nurtured in one of the most reprehensible institutions of crime known to humanity—slavery. During these years blacks had no power over their destiny or sexuality. As a result, Douglass was the son of an unknown white father and Harriet Bailey, a slave. Douglass's mother was never granted the opportunity to raise him herself and would walk several miles to visit him in Talbot County, Maryland. When Douglass was around seven, his mother died, and he later stated that "her death soon ended the little communication that had existed between us; and with it, I believe, a life full of weariness and heartfelt sorrow."[1]

In the absence of parental care, Douglass's grandparents, Betsy and Isaac Bailey, became his caretakers. Betsy watched over Douglass and the other children. Douglass remembered his grandmother as "the mother and father." Under her custody, Douglass did not feel the severity of slavery, and for a while he did not know he was a slave. The positive environment of love, happiness, and a sense of belonging clouded the cruel reality of his enslavement. It also reinforced his worldview. But around the age of eight, this positive environment came to an abrupt end, and his positive worldview turned sour. Learning that his grandmother, her children, and himself were not autonomous, but the possession of "Old Master," was psychologically distressing for Douglass. He witnessed the heartless beatings of his Aunt Esther, the shooting death of other slaves, and the better treatment of animals over human beings as part of the slave system. Douglass wondered about the origin and nature of slavery. He could not understand the brutality of slavery and the cruelty of its overseers. Douglass later wrote, "The very first mental effort that I now remember on my part, was an attempt to solve the mystery, Why am I a slave?... When I saw the slave-driver whip a slave-woman, cut the blood out of her neck, and heard

---

[1] Frederick Douglass, *My Bondage and My Freedom* (New York: Miller, Orton and Mulligan, 1968; Arno Press, 1969) 56–57.

her piteous cries, I went away into the corner of the fence, wept and pondered over the mystery."[2]

Someone told Douglass about God's providence and predestination. Douglass was told that "God up in the sky had made all things, and had made black people to be slaves and white people to be masters. [He] was told too that God was good, and that He knew what was best for everybody."[3] Intuitively, Douglass knew that something was theologically disjointed with this rationalization. He said this idea "came point blank against all his notions of goodness."[4] For the first time, Douglass began to beg the question of God's goodness. He could not accept that slavery and his notion of goodness were compatible. His grandmother, who loved and cared for him, exhibited goodness. What he witnessed of slavery was the opposite of goodness.

Douglass experienced a major turning point in his life when he went to Baltimore, Maryland, to work for the Aulds, his new master and mistress. Sophia Auld began to teach him to read. Douglass excelled in learning the alphabet. When Thomas Auld learned of Douglass's efforts to read, he greatly disapproved, stating that education would spoil Douglass and make him discontent with being a slave. Douglass quickly perceived that education and freedom were somehow related. To hold people in bondage, the enslaved education must be denied, and if the enslaved are allowed education, it must be miseducation in order for oppressors to continue their domination over the enslaved. Oppressors must control the thinking and actions of the enslaved if oppression is to survive. With this insight, Douglass wrote, "To make a contented slave,

---

[2] Frederick Douglass to Thomas Auld, 3 September 1848, in *Anti-Slavery Bugle*, 29 September 1848.
[3] Frederick Douglass, *The Life and Times of Frederick Douglass* (New York: Pathway Press, 1941) 58.
[4] Ibid.

you must have a thoughtless one."[5] Oppressors must narrow the thinking of the oppressed as much as possible to help them adapt to their oppression, and they must do it in such a way that the oppressed will think that the values, culture, and ideas of the oppressor are for their highest good.

Determined to read, Douglass cleverly used his white playmates as instructors and soon learned to read and write. Douglass was greatly indebted to his playmates, and he would discuss slavery with his white friends, who would console him. Never among the white boys did Douglass find one who defended the system of slavery. They believed as Douglass that God never made one person to be a slave to another. In his spare time Douglass would blacken boots to make money. To further his reading skills, Douglass purchased *The Columbian Orator*, which he had heard from some little boys was a book for exhibition. The book was a rich treasure for Douglass. Contained in it was a conversation between a master and slave, which resulted in the release of the slave and the well wishes of the slave master.

The book awakened the intellectual potential of Douglass's mind by giving him not only the tools to argue against slavery, but the vocabulary as well. Reading and reflecting on his predicament, Douglass saw that there was no relationship between God's goodness and slavery, and he concluded that the foundation of slavery was built not by God but by "the pride, the power, and the avarice of [human beings]."[6] Human beings are responsible for the crimes in human history, and "what [human beings] can make, [they] can unmake."[7] Douglass elevated the functional ultimacy of human beings and their activity and placed it squarely on their

---

[5] Douglass, *My Bondage and My Freedom*, 320.
[6] Douglass, *The Life and Times of Frederick Douglass*, 96.
[7] Douglass, *My Bondage and My Freedom*, 90.

shoulders. For whatever needs to be changed or reformed in human history, human action is central and indispensable: "Where we are free to act, we are also free to refrain from acting, and where we are able to say no, we are also able to say yes."[8]

Therefore, Douglass understood that his freedom and the freedom of the oppressed could not be left to chance or miracle and that it would not roll in on the wheels of inevitability; it must be seized by the self-actualizational activity of the oppressed. With this understanding, Douglass felt prepared to challenge any person, black or white, who believed that slavery was designed and orchestrated by God. He said, "I have met, at the south, many good, religious Negro people who was under the delusion that God required them to submit to slavery.... I could entertain no such nonsense at this, and I quite lost my patience when I found a Negro man weak enough to believe such stuff."[9]

At the age of thirteen, Douglass's religious thinking began to develop, and he sought to learn more about human freedom and bondage and why the two coexisted. A white Methodist minister by the name of Hanson convinced Douglass that all humans are sinners in the sight of God and that human bondage was a result of sin. Even though Douglass understood the sinful nature of human beings, the theological problem for him was the hierarchical arrangements of sinners. Since all humans are sinners, who has the moral authority to arrange people into a hierarchy? Why is it that one group of sinners are slaves to another group of sinners that are slave masters? Why is it that one group of sinners has a surplus of power and another is suffering from a deficiency of power? If all humans

---

[8] Cited in John A. O'Brien, *Truths Men Live By* (New York: The MacMillian Company, 1946) 247.

[9] Douglass, *The Life and Times of Frederick Douglass*, 96.

are sinners, does God favor one group of sinners over another? Through critical reflection and analysis, Douglass concluded that God does not favor one human group over another; therefore, to accept slavery because all humans are sinners is to fall prey to paternalistic manipulation.

More and more Douglass began to resist slavery and its particular morality, and it caused him great pain and agony to be caught in it. However, he fought to keep body and soul together in a time when the sociological context of slavery and its regnant theology forced a dichotomy between the two. He felt, as W. E. B. Du Bois later acknowledged, "his twoness,—[a slave, a human being]; two souls, two thoughts, two unreconciled strivings; two warrings ideals in one dark body, whose dogged strength alone keeps it from being torn asunder."[10] Though there were still many unanswered questions, Douglass's ongoing struggle to find answers pushed him deeper into critical reflections and analysis.

At the age of sixteen, Douglass was sent back to the plantation from his childhood to be delivered as property, along with the animals, to the beneficiary of his old master's estate. He was placed in the hands of his new master in St. Michaels, Maryland. Captain Auld, the relative of Thomas Auld, was cruel to his slaves by denying them sufficient food. Douglass found himself stealing to survive and reasoned with himself that his actions were the result of the collective sins of society that robbed him of his liberty and earnings, and that whenever a slave helped him or herself to the master's goods the slave was not stealing, but collecting his due for unpaid labor. Protesting the immorality of the slave system, Douglass said, "Slaveholders made it impossible for the slave to commit any crime, known either to the laws of God or to the laws of

---

[10] W. E. B. DuBois, *The Souls of Black Folks* (Chicago: A.C. McClurg & Co., 1929) 215.

man. If he stole, he but took his own; if he killed his master, he only imitated the heroes of the Revolution."[11] Douglass's internal criticism of the slave system and its particular religious morality was moving him toward a belief and value system that undercut the beliefs, values, and conceptual framework of a religious morality that maintained slavery. Due to the different social location of the master and slave, Douglass's critical insight began to flow out beyond the religious categories that were framed in order to keep him and his people in slavery.

Further distrust of Christianity as practiced in America came when Douglass watched his slave master's religious conversion. Douglass witnessed the redness of his master's face, his disheveled hair, and the teardrop on his cheek. Douglass hoped this outward expression of religion would motivate his master to "emancipate his slave; or, if he should not do so much as this, he will at any rate behave towards [the slaves] more kindly, and feed us more generously than he has heretofore done."[12] But to Douglass's dismay, "if religion had any effect at all on him, it made him more cruel and hateful in all his ways."[13] Douglass viewed the conversion a farce and reached the conclusion that there were two types of religion. One serves as highest good, and the other acts to stifle our highest good by protecting the status quo. This view was reinforced when a mob of leading religious leaders, which included Douglass's master, broke up a Sabbath school started as an aid to slaves who wanted to learn how to read the New Testament. One member of the mob accused Douglass of trying to be another Nat Turner, who had led an insurrection in Virginia. The mob warned Douglass that if he did not accept the status quo, he would be ignominiously executed like Nat

---

[11] Douglass, *The Life and Times of Frederick Douglass*, 102.
[12] Ibid., 122.
[13] Ibid., 123.

Turner. These incidents shook Douglass's confidence in the power of Christianity to make people wiser or better. He saw the inconsistency of the Christianity practiced in America and the Christianity of Christ. The Christianity of Christ serves as our highest good, but the Christianity practiced in America went against our highest good. Douglass said, "Between the Christianity of this land, and the Christianity of Christ, I recognize the widest possible difference—so wide, that to receive the one as good, pure, and holy, is of necessity to reject the other as bad, corrupt, and wicked. To be a friend of the one is of necessity to be the enemy of the other."[14] Douglass understood that one cannot serve two masters. You cannot advocate the cause of the oppressed and at the same time side with the oppressors. To stand for one is to struggle against the other.

Disgusted with Douglass's rebellion as a slave, Captain Auld sent him to Edward Covey, the "Negro-breaker." Upon arrival at Covey's plantation, Douglass was immediately put to work. His work was hard and brought him to exhaustion. In addition to hard work, Douglass was persecuted. For six months, Douglass was beaten, cut, and tormented by Covey. Covey was successful at breaking Douglass. Douglass said, "Mr. Covey succeeded in breaking me—in body, soul, and spirit. My natural elasticity was crushed; my intellect languished...the dark night of slavery closed in upon me, and behold a man transformed into a brute."[15] Pondering over his plight, Douglass questioned the providence of God. He wondered if there was a God, and if there was, why had he not come to his rescue and that of his fellow slaves? Can God's "almightiness" be relied upon? Can liberation be left to chance

---

[14] Frederick Douglass, *Narrative of the Life of Frederick Douglass, an American Slave* (Garden City: Anchor Books, 1973) Appendix, 153.

[15] Douglass, *The Life and Times of Frederick Douglass*, 140.

or miracle? According to Douglass, "Brooding over the singular and mournful lot to which I was doomed, my mind [passed] over the whole scale or circle of belief and unbelief, from faith in the overruling Providence of God, to the purest atheism."[16]

Feeling that he had no friend on earth and doubting if he had one in heaven, Douglass decided to strike the first blow on behalf of his own liberation. He decided his destiny would be in his own hands. His theistic posture of total dependence upon God gave way to a human-centered codetermination, a belief that humans work with God in deciding the course of events in history as a consequence of their freedom that is endowed by God. Douglass resolved to defend himself against the brutality of Covey. Thus, he discarded the slave theology that yielded a quietist response, which was to never strike back at the oppressor and to wait on God for deliverance and that God would take care of everything in his own good time. Douglass said, "My religious views on the subject of resisting my master had suffered a serious shock by the savage persecution to which I had been subjected, and my hands were no longer tied by my religion.... I had backslidden from this point in the slaves' religious creed."[17] Douglass evinced that a particular type of religion can serve the maintenance needs of oppression. Unless the oppressed break from this particular type of religion, they will never counter the forces against them. They will never attain the freedom that they deeply desire. Their religion makes it necessary.

Breaking loose from the kind of religion that results in a resignation to the present social order, Douglass decided to fight back. When Covey tried to beat Douglass again, a fight broke out, and Douglass subdued Covey: "Whereas the

---

[16] Ibid., 147.
[17] Ibid., 139.

violence of the oppressors prevents the oppressed from being fully human, the response of the latter to this violence is grounded in the desire to pursue the right to be human."[18] The fight with Covey transformed Douglass to a man with dignity and self-respect. He was a resurrected person from the tomb of nonbeing. Douglass recalled,

> This battle with Mr. Covey...was the turning point in my life as a slave. It rekindled in my breast the smoldering embers of liberty.... I was nothing before—I was a man now. It recalled to life my crushed self-respect, and my self-confidence, and inspired me with a renewed determination to be a free man.... I felt as I had never felt before. It was a resurrection from the dark and pestiferous tomb of slavery, to the heaven of comparative freedom. I was no longer a servile coward, trembling under the frown of a brother worm of the dust, but my long-cowed spirit was roused to an attitude of independence.... This spirit made me a freeman in fact, though I still remained a slave in form.[19]

When the oppressed struggle against inhumanity, they have a sense of worth and dignity. It is up to the oppressed to snatch back their humanity from those who enslave them.

For several months after the fight with Covey, Douglass was not whipped again. Because he stood up against his oppression and put an end to the brutality to which he had been subjected, he was respected as a man who could be ordered but never again forced to work. Upon leaving the plantation to work for another slave master, Douglass said that

---

[18] Paulo Freire, *Pedagogy of the Oppressed* (New York: Continuum Publishing Company, 1993) 38.

[19] Douglass, *The Life and Times of Frederick Douglass*, 143.

Covey was as "gentle as a lamb." Douglass reclaimed his manhood, confirming that "it is only the oppressed who, by freeing themselves, can free their oppressors.... It is therefore essential that the oppressed wage the struggle to resolve the contradiction in which they are caught; and the contradiction will be resolved by the appearance of the new man: neither oppresssor nor oppressed, but man in the process of liberation."[20]

The desire to be free was still a burning passion within Douglass. Though under a new master, Douglass's plight was very much improved. He never suffered a blow during his stay at Mr. Freeland's farm. Douglass attributed this improved condition to the fact that Freeland was not a religious man. He observed that the more religious the slave owners, the more cruel they were, and vice versa. Speaking about his stay at Freeland's farm, Douglass noted,

> To outward seeming the year at Mr. Freeland's passed off very smoothly. Not a blow was given me during the whole year. To the credit of Mr. Freeland, irreligious though he was, it must be stated that he was the best master I ever had until I became my own master and assumed for myself, as I had a right to do, the responsibility of my own existence and the exercise of my own powers.[21]

Realistically, Douglass knew that he could never be free as long as he could not be the master of his own life. He understood that as long as he operated within set boundaries, he could never achieve a fuller humanity.

Though it was a risky venture, Douglass escaped from slavery in 1838 by impersonating a black sailor who had the

---

[20] Freire, *Pedagogy of the Oppressed*, 38.
[21] Douglass, *The Life and Times of Frederick Douglass*, 153.

permission to move about the country. On 3 September, Douglass arrived in Philadelphia and then went on to New York. He contacted Anna Murray, a free woman from Baltimore whom Douglass had met earlier at the local debating club for free African Americans. Douglass, the sole slave at these gatherings, would debate the issues of life and spend time with Anna, with whom he fell in love. Anna, and Douglass's goal to be the master of his own life, was the driving force behind Douglass's desire to be free. He knew that in order to live life with the woman he loved, he would have to escape from slavery. Anna, who loved Douglass as well, knew that her life would be in danger by marrying a fugitive, but she was willing to take the risk to free Douglass from the jaws of slavery. According to Douglass, Anna was "willing to put her small savings at his command and risk all the dangers and uncertainties of life in the North with a fugitive."[22] Devising a plan to escape from slavery by borrowing a sailor's uniform, Douglass was able to get past the train conductor. Once Douglass reached the free soil of the North, he contacted Anna. They married and moved on to New Bedford, Massachusetts. Douglass tried to find work as a caulker, a skill in which he was trained but could not profit from at all in the South. Though he sought this kind of work up North, white racism prevented him from working at his trade. He held various jobs to keep food on the table and enjoyed working for himself and not giving his earnings to a slave master. To rule one's own life and to chart one's own course are the great glories of liberty, and Douglass relished in it.

---

[22] Corinne K. Hoexter, *Black Crusader: Frederick Douglass* (Chicago: Rand McNally and Company, 1970) 56.

2

DOUGLASS:

AN ELOQUENT VOICE AGAINST

OPPRESSION

As a fugitive up North who could easily be caught and sent back into the jaws of slavery, Douglass had to be careful and watchful. The North was not as wholesome as believed, though it was better than the hell of the South. Douglass witnessed de facto segregation and discrimination and saw how even the free blacks were still oppressed and forced to live on the margin of society. But at least Douglass was able to read and expand his mind without repercussions. The social mistreatment he witnessed of free blacks stimulated his thinking to see that the solution to the problem of oppression is not to "integrate the oppressed into the structure of oppression, but to transform that structure so that they can become beings for themselves."[1]

After less than six months in New Bedford, Douglass subscribed to *The Liberator*, edited by William Lloyd Garrison. Douglass read this paper with great enthusiasm. The paper contained liberating themes that were made absent in the religion he had known before. Douglass said this "paper took a place in my heart second only to the Bible. It detested slavery and made no truce with the traffickers in the bodies and souls of men. It preached human brotherhood; it exposed hypocrisy and wickedness in high places; it denounced oppression, and with all the solemnity of 'Thus saith the Lord,' demanded the complete emancipation of my race."[2] As an avid reader of *The Liberator*, Douglass knew the position of the abolitionists well. He later had the opportunity to hear Garrison speak out against slavery and oppression. It was not long before Douglass was introduced to the abolitionists. During an antislavery convention in Nantucket, Douglass was asked to speak a few words. His words were so powerful and earthshaking that the abolitionists asked him to join them in the crusade to liberate the oppressed. Douglass was put on the payroll, and from that time on he represented an eloquent and burning voice of rebuke to slavery and oppression.

For a while, Douglass traveled with the abolitionists and narrated his story of slavery. Crowds would gather to hear this black man speak on behalf of his cause. The abolitionists who traveled with Douglass, however, wanted him to stay within the confines of narration. One abolitionist, John A. Collins, instructed Douglass to "give us the facts, we will take care of

---

[1] Paulo Freire, *Pedagogy of the Oppressed* (New York: Continuum Publishing Company, 1993) 55.

[2] Frederick Douglass, *The Life and Times of Frederick Douglass* (New York: Pathway Press, 1941) 213.

the philosophy." George Foster said, "People won't believe you ever were a slave, Frederick, if you keep on his way." Collins continued to protest, saying to Douglass, "Better to have a little of the plantation speech than not, it is not best that you seemed too learned."[3] But Douglass was outgrowing this expectation; he could not leave his mind and thoughts under the control of whites, even though these whites were abolitionists seeking the demise of a system he most abhorred. To leave his mind and thoughts under their control would be oppression under a new guise. Douglass said, "No man can be truly free whose liberty is dependant upon the thought, feeling, and actions of others, and who has himself no means in his own hands for guarding, protecting, defending, and maintaining that liberty."[4] What Douglass wanted the white abolitionists to see was that "the oppressed must be their own example in the struggle for their redemption."[5] They must be the ones to construct their own grievances against the system that invalidates their humanity.

Douglass eventually parted with the Garrisonians. One issue that divided Douglass from the Garrisonians was his desire to start his own antislavery newspaper. Many Garrisonians advised Douglass against it, and Garrison himself vehemently opposed it. But Douglass thought his own publication would dispel public stereotype that blacks were inferior and could not stand on their own. Douglass said, "The man who has suffered the wrong is the man to demand redress—the man struck is the man to cry out—and that he who has endured the cruel pangs of slavery is the man to

---

[3] Ibid., 214.
[4] Ibid., 345.
[5] Freire, *Pedagogy of the Oppressed*, 36.

advocate liberty."[6] In the struggle, Douglass wanted to fight for his own cause. He said, "It must be no longer white lawyer and black woodsawyer, white editor, and black street cleaner: it must be no longer white intelligent, and black, ignorant."[7] From Douglass's perspective, the time had come for the oppressed to speak for themselves.

Relocating to the city of Rochester, New York, to prepare the first issue of his own newspaper, Douglass said, "In the publication of the paper, I shall be under no party or society, but shall advocate the slaves' cause in that way which in my judgement, will be best suited to the advancement of the cause."[8] He further stated that "if the colored people will continue to strut about in the mental 'old clothes' of the white race and refuse to think for themselves they will be a disgraced race."[9]

Douglass was still a student of Garrisonian orthodoxy, which taught that political action by voting was unnecessary in the pursuit of liberation, that the Constitution was a proslavery document, and that liberation must come through moral suasion alone. But after he broke with the Garrisonians, Douglass admitted that he uncritically accepted the Garrisonian doctrine and advocated them "with pen and tongue" because he "was bound, not only by their superior knowledge, to take their opinions in respect to this subject, as

---

[6] Frederick Douglass to J. D. Carr, 1 November 1847, in *National Anti-Slavery Standard*, 27 January 1848; *North Star*, 3 December 1847; *North Star*, 22 December 1848.

[7] Philip S. Foner, ed., *The Life and Writings of Frederick Douglass*, vol.1 (New York: International Publishers, 1971) 291.

[8] Ibid., 82-83.

[9] Philip S. Foner, ed., *The Life and Writings of Frederick Douglass*, Vol. 2 (New York: International Publishers, 1971) 360.

the true ones, but also because [he] had no means of showing the unsoundness of these opinions."[10]

As an independent thinker who was developing his own perspective, Douglass determined that he could not avoid the political process. In fact, he now saw it as his duty to exercise his political right as a "powerful means for abolishing slavery." Not to involve himself in the political process would automatically make him a silent endorser of the politics of the status quo. As a black man in America speaking on behalf of his oppressed people, Douglass knew it was not possible to make social changes while remaining politically inactive. As he saw it, oppression is religious *and* political; it is the religion and politics of those who want to continue exercising their power and privilege over the powerless. Unlike his Garrisonian cohorts, who had an apolitical doctrine, Douglass knew the political system was relative and that he must enter it in order to fulfill his mission to liberate his people from their oppression. No longer was there a place for apoliticity in Douglass's thought.

After critically analyzing the U.S. Constitution, Douglass determined it to be an antislavery document. This furthered alienated him from the Garrisonian fold, who saw it as a proslavery document. Douglass wrote about how he came to his new position on the Constitution.

My new circumstances compelled me to re-think the whole subject, and to study with some care not only the just and proper rights, powers, and duties of civil governments, and also the relations which human beings sustain to it. By such a course of thought and reading I was conducted to the conclusion that the Constitution of the United States— inaugurated to 'form a more perfect union, establish justice, insure domestic tranquility, provide for the common defense,

---

[10] Douglass, *The Life and Times of Frederick Douglass*, 261.

promote the general welfare, and secure the blessings of liberty'—could not well have been designed at the same time to maintain, especially as not one word can be found in the Constitution to authorize such a belief.[11]

Nevertheless, Douglass concluded, "The Constitution, in its language and in its spirit, welcomes the black [race] to all the rights which was intended to guarantee to any class of the American people. Its preamble tells us for whom and for what it was made."[12] Douglass's changing views about politics, the Constitution, and the government made him the loose cannon on the abolitionists' ship. A storm of vituperation was leveled against him for his larger critical perspective on the Constitution beyond Garrisonian orthodoxy.

As an oppressed person who was once held in slavery, Douglass's worldview was different from his white abolitionist counterparts. Who is better prepared than the one oppressed to understand and speak against an oppressive society that stifles humanity? Douglass knew oppression and its terrible effects from firsthand experience, and he better understood the necessity for liberation than those who were not enslaved. Douglass discovered how stifling the Garrisonian "school of reformers" was; and he said that it was "too narrow in its philosophy and too bigoted in spirit to do justice to any whom ventured to differ from it."[13] He discovered that many who join the oppressed for their liberation "bring with them the marks of their origin: their prejudices and their deformations, which include a lack of confidence in the people's ability to think, to want, to know."[14] Those who are of the privileged class must

---

[11] Ibid., 261–62.

[12] Philip S. Foner, ed., *The Life and Writings of Frederick Douglass*, vol. 3 (New York: International Publishers, 1972) 354.

[13] Frederick Douglass to Charles Sumner, 2 September 1852, in *The Life and Writings of Frederick Douglass*, 2:210.

[14] Freire, *Pedagogy of the Oppressed*, 42.

never give the oppressed the feeling that they know more about their oppression and its correction than the oppressed who are victimized by it: "The convert who approaches the people but feels alarm at each step they take, each doubt they express, and each suggestion they offer, and attempts to impose his 'status,' remains nostalgic towards his origins."[15] Those who invalidate and dominate the ability of the oppressed in the process of transforming the social order are deceiving themselves. There can be no true transformation of the unjust social situation without the thoughts and actions of the oppressed. To do so would be a farce.

Douglass sought to learn the causes of his suffering and that of his people. He needed to do his own investigation and critical analysis in order to construct a corrective methodology to effectively eradicate the source of oppression. His break with the Garrisonians compelled him to do a more comprehensive appraisal of the religious and political tradition in America to determine its liberation potential. The result of his appraisal was that America was hypocritical and did not practice its creed of freedom. Its Christianity was not Christian, but a religion of oppression. In July 1852, Douglass had the opportunity to point out America's inconsistency in religion and politics, and he did so with great passion and eloquence. In a Fourth of July speech, Douglass railed against the religious and political system of America. Speaking in Rochester, New York, Douglass said,

> Americans! Your republican politics, not less than your religion, are flagrantly inconsistent. You boast of your love of liberty, your superior civilization, and your pure Christianity, while the whole political power of the nation is solemnly pledge to support and perpetuate

---

[15] Ibid., 43.

the enslavement of three million of your countrymen.... The existence of slavery in this country brands your republicanism as a sham, your humanity as a base pretense and your Christianity as a lie. It destroys your moral power abroad: it corrupts your politicians at home. It saps the foundation of religion;...it fetters your progress; it is the enemy of improvement; the deadly foe of education; it fosters pride; it breeds insolence; it promotes vice; it shelters crime; it is a curse to the earth that supports it; and yet you cling to it as if it were the sheet anchor of all your hopes. Oh! Be warned! Be warned! A horrible reptile is coiled up in your nation's bosom; the venomous creature is nursing at the tender breast of your youthful republic; for the love of God, tear away, and fling from you the hideous monster, and let the weight of twenty million crush and destroy it forever![16]

Further indictment came when Douglass asked, "What, to the American slave, is your Fourth of July?" How could a people celebrate a day of freedom and independence when they were held captive by a nation that refused to recognize their humanity? With his thinking grounded in a liberating vision and his spirit touched by the prophets of old, Douglass answered his own question:

I answer; a day that reveals to him, more than all others days in the year, the gross injustice and cruelty to which he is the constant victim. To him, your celebration is a sham; your boasted liberty, an unholy license; your national greatness, swelling vanity; your sounds of rejoicing are empty and heartless; your

---

[16] Frederick Douglass, "The Meaning of July 4th for the Negro," Foner, ed., *Life and Writings*, 2:199, 201.

denunciation of tyrants, brass fronted impudence; your shouts of liberty and equality, hollow mockery; your prayers and hymns, your sermons and thanksgivings, with all your religious parade and solemnity, are, to him, mere bombast, fraud, deception, impiety, and hypocrisy—a thin veil to cover up crimes which would disgrace a nation of savages. There is not a nation on earth guilty of practices more shocking and bloody than are the people of the United States, at this very hour.... Roam through all of the monarchies and despotism of the Old World, travel through South America, search out every abuse, and when you have found the last, lay your facts by the side of the everyday practices of this nation, and you will say with me, that for the revolting barbarity and shameless hypocrisy, America reigns without a rival.[17]

Douglass's constant reading and reflection revealed how grossly Christianity was being misused as a tool for oppression. He heard southern ministers preach that it was the arrangement of Providence that one group of people was made to do the thinking and the other group the working. This arrangement, of course, meant that the black race was not on an equal ontological status with the white race, a stance Douglass saw as nonsensical, a religious maneuvering to keep the slaves docile. The great scheme was clear to Douglass: the slave masters and their divines perpetuated the horrible system of slavery. Douglass said, "Religion and slavery are linked and interlinked with each other—woven and interwoven together.... We have slaveholders as class-leaders, ministers of the Gospel, elders, deacons, doctors of divinity, professors of theology, and even bishops. We have the slave holder in all

---

[17] Ibid., 192.

parts of the church." Douglass discovered that the church was part of the problem. As Alfred North Whitehead said, "The true method of discovery is like the flight of an aeroplane. It starts from the ground of a particular observation; it makes a flight in the thin air of imaginative generalization; and it again lands for renewed observation rendered acute by rational interpretation."[18]

The church could not be trusted; as Douglass witnessed, the church was the guarantor of the system of oppression. It was the entrenchment of a racialized society in which blacks were discriminated against in every way. Oppression formed America's religion, and Douglass was able to comprehend the particular tilt of American Christianity. It certainly was not neutral and impartial; in fact, as Douglass saw it, the church was on the side of oppressors. He saw how American Christianity was contaminated by fraud, deception, and hypocrisy. Its whole theoretical framework was designed to perpetuate oppression; as a man in search of a theological perspective conducive to liberation, Douglass labored tenaciously to show that American Christianity was antihuman and diametrically opposed to the prophets of old and the gospel of Jesus Christ. He knew the biblical message meant liberation not only from the chains of slavery, but from the functional theological framework of a religion that splits humanity into two groups and arranges them into a hierarchy of masters and slaves, males and females, superior and inferior, with the claim that God set it up and, therefore, it is right, moral, and just.

Equally important is Douglass's understanding that the true gospel of Christ is for the poor and the oppressed. They are the object of God's love and concern embodied in the

---

[18] Alfred North Whitehead, *Process and Reality* (New York: MacMillan Publishing Co., Inc., 1978) 5.

Great Redeemer who came to "preach the gospel to the poor...to heal the broken hearted, to preach deliverance to the captives, and the recovering of sight to the blind, to set at liberty them that are bruised." Believing this about the gospel of Christ, Douglass said,

> Thanks be to God, while under the driver's lash, God in his mercy led me to the knowledge of the scriptures. I gained sufficient [knowledge] of Christianity to know that it had no fellowship with slavery;—I learned enough to satisfy me that he who came to preach deliverance to the captive, he who poured out his blood on Calvary, cared for my rights,—cared for me equally with any white master, and that, so far from his sanctioning the system of slavery, the whole tenor of his life, and of his teaching, were utterly opposed to that system. Believing this, I did not hesitate for a moment to seize the first opportunity, which offered, to gain for myself the freedom for which my soul panted.[19]

Understanding God's will to freedom for all humanity, Douglass moved to the other side of the theological spectrum because the dominant religion and its theology worked at cross-purposes with the will of God and the goal of liberation. The psychological confusion that had once baffled Douglass about his plight had now ceased. He had unraveled the mystery:

> All efforts I had previously made to secure my freedom, had not only failed, but had seemed only to rivet my fetters the more firmly and to render my

[19] John W. Blassingame, *The Frederick Douglass Papers* Series One: Speeches, Debates, and Interviews, Volume 1, 1841–1846 (New Haven: Yale University Press, 1979) 328–29.

escape more difficult. Baffled, entangled and discouraged, I had at times asked myself the question, May not my condition after be God's work and ordered for a wise purpose, and if so, was not submission my duty? A contest had in fact been going on in my mind for a long time, between the clear consciousness of right and the plausible make shift of theology and superstition. The one held me an abject slave—a prisoner for life, punished for some transgression in which I had no lot or part; the other counseled me to manly endeavor to secure my freedom. This contest was now ended; my chains were broken, and the victory brought me unspeakable joy.[20]

The enlightenment of the Scriptures and the particular tilt of the gospel put Douglass at odds with the American cultural way of life. He knew "it was dangerous to let the slave understand that the life and teaching of Jesus meant freedom for the captive and release for those held in economic, social, and political bondage,"[21] yet Douglass' life was consumed with replacing American Christianity of human captivity with the biblical gospel of human liberation. He would not accept any rationalization for slavery and oppression. American Christianity was too corrupt, too bloody, too racist, too sexist, and too filled with iniquity to compromise the truth of the gospel of Christ. The two are incompatible, and Douglass hated with a passion "the corrupt, slaveholding, women-whipping, cradle-plundering, partial and hypocritical [religion]

---

[20] Douglass, *The Life and Times of Frederick Douglass*, 225.
[21] Howard Thurman, *Deep River and the Negro Spiritual Speaks of Life and Death* (Indiana: Friends United Press, 1975) 16.

of this land"[22] because it advocated keeping the slave chains on rather than taking them off.

Perceptive of the concrete oppression that weighed him and his people down and the power that forced them to live in a situation of injustice, Douglass described his mission and call of duty, championing the hopes and aspirations of a people yearning to be free from their oppression. He said,

> This is my object. So long as the slave clinks his chains in bondage, while he lifts up his imploring hands to heaven, and the advocates of freedom everywhere are doing their utmost in his behalf, in exposing his wrongs, and making known the outrages under which he suffers, while I see this, I cannot do other than pursue the course which I am now doing.[23]

Douglass sought to show theologically that any analysis of the gospel that shows anything different or less than God's intention of liberation of the oppressed is unchristian. Even when white Christians tried to use pseudoscientific evidence and to show biblically that dark skin was a curse because "God cursed Ham and therefore American slavery is right," Douglass countered this argument:

> Every year brings with it multitudes of this class of slaves [slaves of white fathers]. It was doubtless in consequence of knowledge of this fact, that one great statesman of the south predicted the downfall of slavery by the inevitable laws of population. Whether this prophecy is ever fulfilled or not, it is nevertheless plain that a very different-looking class of people are springing up at the south, and are now held in slavery,

---

[22] Frederick Douglass, *Narrative of the Life of Frederick Douglass, an American Slave* (New York: Penguin Books, 1982) 153.

[23] Blassingame, *The Frederick Douglass Papers*, 1:325.

from those originally brought to this country from Africa; and if their increase will do no other good, it will do away the force of the argument, that God cursed Ham, and therefore American slavery is right. If the lineal descendants of Ham are alone to be scripturally enslaved, it is certain that slavery at the south must soon become unscriptural.[24]

Through his newspaper publications, autobiographies, and public speeches, Douglass seized every opportunity to crush the Christian enterprise of slavery and the theological, philosophical, and scientific rationale for maintaining it. Though it was dangerous and unpopular to go against public opinion concerning slavery, Douglass knew he had to guard against falsehood, dogmatism, and outright superstition in the struggle to liberate the oppressed. When people argued that blacks were naturally inferior to whites, Douglass vehemently rejected this falsehood:

Inferior race! This is the apology, the philosophical and ethnological apology for all the hell-black crimes ever committed by the white race against the blacks and the warrant for the repetition of those crimes through all times. Inferior race!... I should like to know what constitutes inferiority and the standard of superiority. Must a man be as wise as Socrates must, as learned as Humbolt, as profound as Bacon, or as eloquent as Charles Sumner, before he can be reckoned among superior men? Alas! If this were so, few even of the most cultivated of the white race could stand the test. Webster was white and had a large head, but all white men have not large heads. The Negro is black and has a small head, but all Negroes have not small heads. What

---

[24] Douglass, *Narrative of the Life of Frederick Douglass*, 50.

rule shall we apply to all these heads? Why this: Give all an equal chance to grow.[25]

In his quest to liberate the oppressed and find a theological perspective that would not work at cross-purposes with liberation, Douglass was willing to dump and discard any idea, belief, and body of material that served the maintenance needs of oppression and stifled the movement toward liberation. He would even disregard the Bible if he was ever convinced that it was proslavery:

> I do not believe that the Bible sanctions American slavery.... But here I will say, that should the doctors of divinity ever convince me that the Bible sanctions American slavery, that Christ and his apostles justify returning men to bondage, then will I give the Bible to the flames, and no more worship God in the name of Christ. For of what value to men would a religion be which not only permitted, but enjoined upon the enslavement of each other, and which would leave them to sway of physical force, and permit the strong to enslave the weak?[26]

Anything that stood in the way of the liberation of the oppressed or invalidated human rights, no matter how sacred the name it bore, Douglass was there to challenge it. Since the church and its religious leaders were willing to continue serving the interest of slavery and oppression through their religious practices and interpretations, Douglass was just as willing to opt for atheism or anything that would repudiate and overthrow the system of slavery. Attacking the practice of Christianity in America, Douglass thundered,

---

[25] Foner, ed., *The Life and Writings of Frederick Douglass*, 3:355–56.
[26] Foner, ed., *The Life and Writings of Frederick Douglass*, 2:284.

For my part, I would say, welcome infidelity! welcome atheism! welcome anything! In preference to the gospel, as preached by the Divines! They convert the very name of religion into an engine of tyranny and barbarous cruelty, and serve to confirm more infidels, in this age, than all the infidel writings of Thomas Paine, Voltaire, and Bolingbroke put together have done! These ministers make religion a cold and flintyhearted thing, having neither principles of right actions nor bowels of compassion. They strip the love of God of its beauty and leave the throne of religion a huge, horrible, repulsive form. It is a religion for oppressors, tyrants, manstealers, and thugs.... [It] favors the rich against the poor; which exalts the proud above the humble; which divides mankind into two classes, tyrants, and slaves; which says to the man in chains, stay there; and to the oppressor, oppress on; it is a religion which may be professed and enjoyed by all the robbers and enslavers of mankind; it makes God a respecter of persons, denies his fatherhood of the race, and tramples in the dust the great truth of the brotherhood of man.[27]

It was not that Douglass hated religion. He valued it, but he had to quarantine American Christianity because it was instrumental in maintaining oppression. Douglass saw the link between specific attitudes toward suffering and the maintenance needs of oppression. For example, the interpretive framework of American Christianity taught the slaves that they were inferior and that whites were superior. This type of preaching and teaching, Douglass said, "is the ignorance in which the slaves are held that some of them go home and say, 'me hear a good sermon to day, de minister make ebery thing

---

[27] Ibid., 377–78.

so clear, white man above a nigger any day.'" Douglass viewed this as a clear example of antipowerism promoted by the oppressor to keep the oppressed in their place. The worthiness and equality of the enslaved would never be validated until the oppressed move away from seeing the world through Eurocentric paradigms. Their mental health depended upon their willingness to debut the misreligion they had been taught, and it was this misreligion that Douglass rallied against and desperately worked to replace with the gospel of Jesus Christ.

Douglass evinced the difference between the religion he hated and the one he desperately wanted to put in its place:

> I love religion—I love the religion of Jesus, which is pure and peaceable, and easy to be entreated. I ask you to love this religion; but I hate a religion which, in the name of the Saviour, prostitutes his blessed precepts to the vile purposes of slavery, ruthlessly sunders all the ties of nature, which tears the wife from the husband—which separates the child from the parent—which covers the backs of men and women with bloody scars—which promotes all manner of licentiousness. I hate such a religion as this, for it is not Christianity—it is of the devil. I ask you to hate it too, and to assist me in putting in its place the religion of Jesus.[28]

For Douglass, the religion of Jesus was the true religion; Jesus was an advocate of freedom and a catalyst for the economic, social, and political uplift of the downtrodden. Douglass was willing to give his allegiance to this religion because it was the opposite of the religion practiced in America, which justified and supported the status quo. By contrast, Douglass said,

---

[28] Blassingame, *The Frederick Douglass Papers*, 1:35.

There is another religion. It is that which takes off the fetters instead of binding them on—that breaks every yoke—that lifts up the bowed down.... It spreads its table to the lame, the halt, and the blind. It goes down after a long neglected race. It passes, link by link till it finds the lowest link in humanity's chain—humanity's most degraded form in the most abject condition. It reaches down its arm and tells them to stand up.... This is Christianity.[29]

However, American Christianity could not pass the test of this gospel. It was greatly lacking in giving justice to the oppressed by breaking their chains and letting the captives free. It was a religion of the devil, which pillaged and exploited the powerless. Douglass saw no liberation coefficient in the religion that was practiced in America for the oppressed, except, of course, the eschatological; and Douglass was unwilling to spiritualize oppression and relegate liberation to eschatological compensation for the suffering of slavery because such compensation did nothing to improve conditions here and now. In protest, Douglass gave this advice to his oppressed people who had escaped from the jaws of slavery:

If you would will join a...church, let it not be one which approves of the Negro-pew, and which refuses to treat slaveholding as a high crime against God and man. It were better, that you sacrifice your lives than by going into the Negro-pew, you invade your self-respect—debase your souls—play the traitor to your race—and crucify afresh Him who died for the one brotherhood of man.

---

[29] Ibid., vol. 2:1847–1854, 101. John Blassingame, *The Frederick Douglass Papers*. 2:1847-54 (New Haven and London: Yale University Press, 1979-1985) 101.

Join no political party, which refuses to commit itself fully, openly, and heartfully, in its newspaper, meetings, and nominations, to the doctrine, that slavery is the grossest of all absurdities, as well as the guiltiest of all abominations, and that there can no more be a law for the enslavement of man, made in the image of God, than for the enslavement of God himself. Vote for no man for civil office, who makes your complexion a bar to political, ecclesiastic or social equality. Better die than insult yourself and insult our social equality. Better die than insult yourself and insult every person of African blood, and insult your Maker, by contributing to elevate to civil office he who refuses to eat with you, to sit by your side in the House of Worship, or to let his children sit in the school by the side of your children.[30]

Douglass would not accept any religion or be a part of any political party that refused to grant total freedom and equality to the oppressed. In his comprehensive appraisal of American Christianity and its theological norms that controlled its interpretive framework, Douglass found it to be oppressive, and this is the reason he was opposed to giving Bibles to the slaves. Thus, he said,

First give us ourselves and then we will get Bibles. What the slave begs for is his freedom and the American and Foreign Anti-Slavery Society comes forward and says, 'Here is a Bible....' For my part I am not for giving the slave the Bible or anything else this side of his freedom. Give him that first and then you need not give him anything else. He can get what he

---

[30] Philip S. Foner, ed., *The Life and Writings of Frederick Douglass*, vol. 5 (New York: International Publishers, 1975) 167–68.

needs.... Now what we want is to first give the slave
himself. God did not say to Moses "Tell my people to
serve me that they may go free," but "Go and tell
Pharaoh to let my people go that they may serve me."
The first thing is freedom. It is the all-important thing.
There can be no virtue without freedom—there can be
no obedience to the Bible without freedom.[31]

Douglass understood that the first plea of the oppressed is
liberation. Without liberation, everything else is in a stifling
state of affairs. It would do the enslaved no good to own Bibles
when they could not first own themselves. Slavery and
oppression affected the way the enslaved serve God. They
could not possibly carry out the mandates of the gospel when
they were held in bondage against their will. Without
liberation first, religion is elusive and becomes superstitious.
Too much wrong had already been done in the name of
religion, and Douglass labored for nothing less than the
liberation of the oppressed. He would rather the oppressed be
free than make claims to a religion. Freedom is the right to
choose in life, and religion cannot substitute for that right:
"Freedom is not an ideal located outside of [the oppressed]; nor
is it an idea which becomes myth. It is rather the indispensable
condition for the quest for human completion."[32]

Douglass was very suspicious of religion, especially the
religion of the oppressor, which constantly devalued the
humanity of the oppressed and resulted in their resignation to
the present social order. In fact, he thought this was one of the
major reasons for slavery and oppression in America. Religion
had become the guarantor of unjust social situations. It had
aided and abetted in keeping oppression alive and guaranteeing

---

[31] Foner, ed., *The Life and Writings of Frederick Douglass*, Vol. 2, 182-183.
[32] Freire, *Pedagogy of the Oppressed*, 29.

its continued disguise. As Douglass saw it, there was too much religion of a certain type that had dried up the springs of human compassion and starved the land of love. Douglass voiced his suspicions about too much religion:

I believe the grand reason why we have slavery in this land at the present moment is that we are too religious as a nation, in other words,...we have substituted religion for humanity—we have substituted a form of Godliness, an outside show for the real thing itself. We have houses built for the worship of God, which are regarded as too sacred to plead the cause of the downtrodden million in them. They tell you in these churches that they are willing to receive you to talk to them about sins of the Scribes and Pharisees, or on the subject of the heathenism of the South Sea Islands, or on any of the subjects connected with missions, the Tract Society, the Bible Society, and other Societies connected with the Church, but the very moment you ask them to open their mouths for the liberation of the southern slaves, they tell you, that is a subject with which they have nothing to do, and which they do not wish to have introduced into the church.[33]

Seeing that the church reflected the unjust ethos of the times, Douglass castigated it. The church was the arch-supporter of the status quo. A church that cannot plead the cause of the oppressed is not the true ecclesia, and Douglass could not give it support or respect. Because his theological perspective was diametrically opposed to the passive acquiescence and corrupt practices of the church, Douglass had to stand outside of the church to help create a climate that would lead to the liberation of the oppressed. In one of his speeches, Douglass appealed to an Ohio congregation to join the struggle to liberate the oppressed:

---

[33] Foner, ed., *The Life and Writings of Frederick Douglass,* 2:180.

There must be a struggle to unmask the hypocrisy of those who profess to love God, and yet hate man. The war must be carried into the church. The church is the light of the world. There are individuals out of the church frequently who seize the torch of God's truth and outstrip the multitude, even the church remains behind. But the church is still the light of the world.... The church has remained on the side of slavery, and is linked, and interwoven with slavery, she has bolted her doors, barred her gates against anti-slavery truth.... The church must be opposed, in this enterprise. Necessity compels us to do it, we attack it because we feel it is our duty.[34]

Instead of being a stepping stone to attain liberation, the church was a stumbling block, and Douglass refused to link himself with the church and the theological concepts and beliefs that had caused the oppressed to accept their oppression. Douglass said,

One of the most saddening results of the circumstances of our people is, that they tend to destroy our own faith in ourselves. Having seen ourselves oppressed, despised, and hated for so many long and bitter years, we come at last to think that degradation is our doom. Instead of attributing our condition to the injustice and oppression which have been heaped upon us, we sink down into the belief that we are the victims of our natural inferiority.[35]

---

[34] Cited from "Brilliant Thoughts and Important Truth: A Speech of Frederick Douglass," 1852 in Ohio edited by Larry Gara, Professor of History and Government at Wilmington College, 5.

[35] Foner, ed., *The Life and Writings of Frederick Douglass*, 3:212.

Douglass understood that "the more the oppressed can be led to adapt to that situation, the more easily they can be dominated."[36]

Unless the consciousness of the oppressed shifts from the consciousness of their oppressors, their movement toward liberation is imaginary rather than real. Douglass was well aware that the oppressed had been brainwashed in the theological concepts of their oppressors, making the liberation struggle all the more difficult. Many of the slaves were indoctrinated with the belief that their predicament was part of some divine plan and that liberation would come in God's own time. As one who was not willing to accept this theological idea as factual and who was not willing to rely on Christian theism, Douglass countered it in non-supernatural terms:

> Look not for miracles. We are not expecting to see the waters roll asunder, and give to those now in bondage a dry road to freedom, and then roll back again and swallow up the pursuing hosts of our modern Pharaohs; we are not expecting manna from heaven to satisfy the hunger of the emancipated, nor water to gush forth from the solid rock to quench their thirst. We have to deal with the stubborn facts, and fixed laws, and to regulate our conduct in light of their certain operation. Nothing should be left to chance or to accident.... Our faith is at once to be suspected the moment it leads us to fold our hands and leave the cause of the slave to Providence.... It has been the standing excuse for inaction.... No doctrine is more grateful to the heart of the slaveholder, than that which leave slavery to Divine Providence.[37]

---

[36] Freire, *Pedagogy of the Oppressed*, 55.

[37] Foner, ed., *The Life and Writings of Frederick Douglass*, 3:112.

The key to motivating the oppressed to act on their own behalf is to change their consciousness. Douglass understood that if the oppressed did not shake loose from the oppressor consciousness, the result would be social quietism and continued oppression. The task of anyone who wants to liberate a people is to get them to rid themselves of the internalization of their oppression. Douglass's work was cut out for him, and he labored arduously to free the mind of the oppressed from a distorted view of God's intrusion into human history to set the oppressed free. The beliefs, values, and concepts that the oppressed embrace have contributed to reconciling them to their suffering. Douglass said,

In my communication with the Negro people I have endeavored to deliver them from the power of superstition, bigotry, and priest-craft. In theology I have found them strutting about in the old clothes of the masters, just as the masters strut about in the old clothes of the past. The failing power remains among them long since it has ceased to be the religious fashion in our refined and elegant white churches. I have taught that the "fault is not in our stars, but in ourselves, that we are underlings" that "who would be free, themselves must strike the blow."... My views at this point receive but limited endorsement among my people. They, for the most part, think they have means of procuring special favor and help from the Almighty; and, as their "faith is the substance of things hoped for and the evidence of things not seen", they find much in this expression which is true to faith, but utterly false to fact.[38]

Douglass knew that to achieve liberation, it is first necessary to do some theological housecleaning. Certain theological concepts needed dumping so that a new construction of ideas could be implemented to speed up the

---

[38] Douglass, *The Life and Times of Frederick Douglass*, 529.

process of "setting the captives free." For instance, Douglass removed God's overruling sovereignty from human history and replaced it with human sovereignty over human history. He wanted the oppressed to understand that liberation cannot be left to chance or divine providence, and prayer can never be a substitute for human action; nor can faith alone break one chain, feed the hungry, clothe the naked, and shelter the homeless. There are fixed laws in the universe that are not going to alter because the oppressed are waiting for divine intervention. The intervention of God comes through the actions of human beings. The key to human liberation and social reform is in the hands of humanity itself. Douglass said,

> It seems to me that the true philosophy of reform is not found in the clouds, or in the stars, or anywhere else outside of humanity itself. So far as the laws of the universe have been discovered and understood, they seem to teach that the mission of man's improvement and perfection has been wholly committed to man himself. So is he to be his own savior or his own destroyer. He has neither angels to help him nor devils to hinder him.[39]

For Douglass, the only way progress and reform could be achieved was through a revolution, and if there was to be a revolution, it could only happen when there was a revolution in human beings to be free. Since this is a non-supernatural world in which God does not overrule the decisions of humans, Douglass wanted the oppressed to see that there was no power outside of humans that could bring reform to the world—for this resides in human hands. The future of the world depends

---

[39] *The Frederick Douglass Papers*, "It Moves," Washington: Library of Congress, 1976 (manuscript Division, Microfilm 28:18).

upon humans, and they can work to save it or destroy it, lead it to redemption or perdition. The choice is humanity's to make.

Douglass saw that human activity is central for one's salvation or liberation. Divine power has never removed evil from the world. Without human activity, the low and vile in this world will continue to gain victory over the good and the spiritual side of humanity. Social reform is impossible apart from human participation. Douglass believed that the oppressed must maximize their efforts toward achieving freedom. He pressed this point in his philosophy of reform:

> Let me give you a word of the philosophy of reform. The whole history of the progress of human liberty shows that all concessions yet made to her august claims have been born of earnest struggle. The conflict has been exciting, agitating, all-absorbing, and for the time being, putting all other tumults to silence. It must do this or it does nothing. If there is no struggle there is no progress. Those who profess to favor freedom and yet depreciate agitation, are men who want crops without plowing up the ground, they want rain without thunder and lightning. They want the ocean without the awful roar of its many waters.
>
> This struggle may be a moral one, or it may be a physical one, and it may be both moral and physical, but it must be a struggle. Power concedes nothing without a demand. It never did and it never will. Find out just what any people will submit to and you have found out the exact measure of injustice and wrong which will be imposed upon them, and these will continue till they are resisted with either words or blows, or with both. The limits of tyrants are prescribed by the endurance of those whom they oppress. In the light of these ideas, Negroes will be hunted at the

North, and held and flogged at the South so long as they submit to those devilish outrages, and make no resistance, either moral or physical. Men may not get all they pay for in this world, but they must certainly pay for all they get. If we ever get free from oppressions and wrongs heaped upon us, we must pay for their removal. We must do this by labor, by suffering, by sacrifice, and if needs be, by our lives and the lives of others.[40]

Douglass's commentary on the philosophy of social reform illuminates one unambiguous conclusion: humans in general and the oppressed in particular must look to themselves as the only source of liberation. Human progress and liberation have never been achieved apart from the actions and struggles of humans, and Douglass realized that slavery would not end by some divine power that would force people or nations to chart another course.

Therefore, Douglass opted for counter-violence as a liberation tactic to stop a human tyrannical force. Revolutionary violence was necessary because, as Douglass noted, "It is plain that for the present no race of men can depend upon moral means for the maintenance of their rights.... The only way open to any race to make their rights respected is to learn how to defend them. When it is seen that black men no more than white men can be enslaved with impunity, men will be less inclined to enslaved and oppress them."[41] Douglass was convinced that counter-violence in defense of liberty is justified. Resistance to evil is a moral obligation. Those who believe in justice and don't wage any

---

[40] John Blassingame, *The Frederick Douglass Papers*, series Three, Speeches, Debates, and Interviews, Vol. 3, 1855-63 (New Haven: Yale University Press, 1985) 204.

[41] Foner, ed., *The Life and Writings of Frederick Douglass*, 3:342.

action to stop the evil that is destroying the republic are actually cooperating with it. Douglass was convinced that radical revolutionary activity was the only option left if the oppressed were to achieve freedom and justice. In fact, he saw revolution in this instance no different than the revolution the Founding Fathers waged when they were oppressed by the British government:

> Oppression makes a wise man mad. Your fathers were wise men, and if they did not go mad, they became restive under this treatment.... They were peaceful men; but they preferred revolution to peaceful submission to bondage. They were quiet men; but they did not shrink from agitating against oppression....
>
> They believed in order; but not in the order of tyranny. With them, nothing was settled that was not right. With them, justice, liberty and humanity were final not slavery and oppression.[42]

By no means did Douglass think that the problem of oppression would solve itself with time. This grievous problem can only be solved by the active and immediate action of those who love justice, liberty, and humanity. Douglass believed that no people or nation, Christian or non-Christian, should accept their oppression without resistance: "Nonresistance forms no part of the creed of Christian or Heathen nations. All believe in the right to fight—under certain so-called justifiable circumstances. Freedom is valued not only for its intrinsic worth, but for what it costs."[43]

As pointed out earlier, Douglass's fight with Covey was an open act of resisting evil. Covey, who was the personification

---

[42] Foner, *Life and Writings*, 2:199.
[43] John Blassingane, *The Frederick Douglass Papers, Vols 1-3*, "William, the Silent," (New Haven and London: Yale University Press, 1979-85) 1.

of the evil system of slavery, used violence to subdue Douglass, and Douglass used counter-violence to keep Covey from subduing him. The fight resulted into this: Douglass seized his manhood from the jaws of slavery and transferred his destiny from the overruling sovereignty of the divine to the exalted status of man himself—this is a view similar to humanism. This view motivated Douglass to fight back, and the use of counter-violence is an allowable or legitimate aspect of God's work in a context of overcoming economic, social, and political oppression.

Douglass saw that violence was central in securing justice for the enslaved. When moral persuasion has been exulted, then violence must be employed to secure justice and to have a fuller humanity. Akin to Douglass's understanding of violence is Enrique Dussel's, who describes how Argentina came into being through the use of violence:

When Cain killed Abel, he set up a "totality" in which the other came to be at best a slave under his domination. Everything goes well so long as the slave does not advert to his situation or feel any self-worth. If I feel I am worth nothing, it is because I have been subjected to a pedagogy that has driven that point home to me. But if I suddenly begin to think that I am worth something, if I suddenly place myself outside the totality fashioned by my master and oppressor, then a process of liberation begins and the situation becomes quite serious. The oppressor will try to prevent me from taking the step to freedom; he will try to keep me in his totality by force. This is what Dom Helder Camara calls the "first violence." It is the violence of an unjust situation, which prevents the reified man from being free. This first sin is the gravest of all because it reifies human beings, turning them into things. The person en route to freedom, the person in the "exodus," must defend himself from this first violence.

The defense is just. It seeks to prevent the exercise of a violence that would keep the process of liberation from taking place.... So there is a "first violence": organized, legal violence. And there is a "second" violence: the violence that sets out to establish a new "whole." The second violence is the violence of San Martin, for example. He organized his soldiers and followers. When the Spaniards came to destroy the new homeland, he went out to fight them paving the way for a new whole that is present-day Argentina. If that conflict had not taken place, there would not be any Argentina today.[44]

With this understanding, we can see why Douglass opted for counter-violence. The first violence was already set up, legal, and organized, making the second violence necessary for the creation of a new whole. Douglass realized that in order for the new whole to exist, it must be forced into being or otherwise the first violence will continue to grow in great proportion. Convinced of this, Douglass asserted,

A man without force is without the essential dignity of humanity. Human nature is so constituted, that it cannot honor a helpless man, although it can pity him; and even this it cannot do long, if the signs of power do not arise.... When a slave cannot be flogged he is more than half free. He has a domain as broad as

[44] Enrique Dussel, *History and the Theology of Liberation: A Latin American Perspective*, translated by John Drury (Maryknoll NY: Orbis Books, 1976) 125–27.

his own manly heart to defend, and he is really "a power on earth."[45]

Furthermore, "a man who will not fight for himself, when he has the means of doing so, is not worthy of being fought for by others."[46]

Resolved, and on a larger scale, Douglass knew that slavery would have to end in blood. Douglass stated "that slavery could only be destroyed by bloodshed." His belief in the ultimacy of humans brought him to this conclusion. What humans do on behalf on their own freedom will determine the outcome. Though it is God's will that all are free, humans are the key in making this a reality. Douglass said,

> There is no power in the world which can be relied upon to help the weak against the strong or the simple against the wise; that races, like individuals, must stand or fall by their own merits; that all the prayers of Christendom cannot stop the force of a single bullet, divest arsenic of poison, or suspend any law of nature.... What men sow they will reap, and that there is no way to dodge or circumvent the consequences of any act or deed.[47]

Ultimately, human progress and reform are in human hands, and nothing can be left to a fatalistic reliance on force beyond us.

In a speech to his oppressed bondmen during the Civil War, Douglass urged them to join in the moral revolution "and smite with death the power that would bury the government

---

[45] Frederick Douglass, *My Bondage and My Freedom* (New York: Arno Press, 1969) 246–47.

[46] Philip S. Foner, ed., *The Voice of Black America* (New York: Simon & Schuster, 1972) 198.

[47] Douglass, *The Life and Times of Frederick Douglass*, 529.

and your liberty in the same hopeless grave."[48] Douglass believed that the oppressed must take part in their own liberation because "no people, to whom liberty is given, can hold it as firmly and wear it as grandly as those who wrench their liberty from the iron hand of the tyrant. The hardships and dangers involved in the struggle give strength and toughness to the character, and enable it to stand firm in storm as well as in sunshine."[49] Douglass believed that those who are oppressed must themselves fight in the struggle for liberation. They must be in the process of fighting to regain their stolen humanity. Their future depends upon what they do in the present. Not to engage in the redemption of their situation means they forfeit the opportunity to eliminate oppression and alienation that will continue to impact them and their posterity.

---

[48] Cited in *Negro Orators and Their Orations*, Frederick Douglass, Carter G. Woodson, ed., "Men of Color to Arms," 254.

[49] Douglass, *The Life and Times of Frederick Douglass*, 670.

3

DOUGLASS ATTACKS THE MAINTENANCE NEEDS OF OPPRESSION: RACISM, SEXISM, BELIEFS, AND VALUES

The Civil War was one of the darkest periods in American history. The divide over slavery set the nation at odds with itself. Paternalism and its religious justification were now threatened. Christian abolitionists vigorously stepped up their attack on slavery through literature and public discourse, fanning the winds of militancy to bring about slavery's demise. Douglass was at the forefront of this atmosphere of militancy. The war he advocated would be long and bloody. Nevertheless, Douglass urged President Lincoln to draft and sign the Emancipation Proclamation. Without freedom for all, there could be no nation. The legislation was signed into law, bringing an end to legalized slavery. The North finally conquered the South to bring them into compliance with the federal law. The struggle to end legalized slavery did not come without a price, however. Thousands lost their lives, and others were maimed for life.

But Douglass was not satisfied with the abolition of slavery; he wanted the full citizenship rights of black people, and he felt his work was not completely done until his newly freed people could have the ballot:

> Though slavery was abolished, the wrongs of my people were not ended. Though they were not slaves they were not yet free....
>
> I, therefore, soon found that the Negro had still a cause, and that he needed my voice and pen with others to plead for it.... I felt that the work of the Anti-Slavery Society was not done, that it had not fulfilled its mission, which was not merely to emancipate, but to elevate the enslaved class...the freedman should have the ballot.[1]

There were many who felt they had done enough for the oppressed. The Anti-Slavery Society wanted to dismantle, and others felt the country should focus its attention on something else. Douglass understood that enough had not been done. He knew that the playing field was not leveled, and he fought to reverse this "done enough for the oppressed" sentiment:

> It is said by some: "We have done enough for the Negro." Yes, you have done a great deal for the Negro, and for one, I am deeply sensible for it, and grateful for

---

[1] Frederick Douglass, *The Life and Times of Frederick Douglass* (New York: Pathway Press, 1941) 384–86.

it. But, after all, what have you done? We were slaves—and you have made us free—and given us the ballot. But the world has never seen any people turned loose to such destitution, as were the four million slaves of the south. The old roof was pulled down over their heads before they could make for themselves a shelter. They were free! Free to hunger; free to the winds and rains of heaven; free to the pitiless wrath of enraged masters, who since they could no longer control them, were willing to see them starve. They were free, without roofs to cover them, or bread to eat, or land to cultivate, and as a consequence died in such numbers as to awaken the hope of their enemies that they would soon disappear. We gave them freedom and famine at the same time. The marvel is that they still live. What the Negro wants is, first, protection of the rights already conceded by law, and secondly, education. Talk of having done enough for these people after two hundred years of enforced ignorance and stripes is absurd, cruel, and heartless.[2]

Douglass wanted to impress upon people that there was more to do. Simply turning people loose after 200 years of slavery was not enough. Social programs needed to be put into place to lift up the enslaved from their long years of oppression. They deserved rights to all civil liberties. Those who thought their work was done did not know what was taking place in the South: "In the south, the school-house is burned. Today in Tennessee, Lucy Haydon is called from an inner room at midnight and shot down because she teaches colored children to read. Today in New Orleans and in

---

[2] Philip S. Foner, ed., *The Life and Writings of Frederick Douglass*, Vol. 4 (New York: International Publishers, 1950 – 1975) 96.

Louisiana, and in parts of Alabama, the black man scarcely dares to deposit the votes which you gave him a right to deposit for fear of his life."[3] Until social oppression of this nature was corrected, Douglass knew that the liberation struggle was not over.

On another front, Douglass had to contend with the black clergy, who criticized Douglass for not giving thanks to God for the successful overthrow of slavery. In a powerful rebuke, Douglass said,

> I dwell here in no hackneyed cant about thanking God for this deliverance.... I object to it largely, because I find that class of men who have done nothing for the abolition of slavery themselves, and would do nothing for the abolition of slavery, but led everything against the abolition of slavery, always holding us back by telling us that God would abolish slavery in his own good time. So they want us to join them in thanking God for the deliverance.
>
> God has given to man certain great powers, and man, in the exercise of these great powers, is to work out his own salvation—the salvation of society—eternal justice, goodness, mercy, wisdom, knowledge, with these gospels of God to reform mankind, and my thanks tonight are to willing hearts and the willing hands that labored in the beginning, amid loss of reputation, amid insult and martyrdom, and at imminent peril of life and limb. My thanks are to those brave spirits who in an evil hour had the courage and devotion to remember and

---

[3] Ibid., 96.

stand by the cause of liberty, and to demand the emancipation of the bondmen.[4]

Douglass was often critical of the black church and its ministers. He thought that the energy put into spiritualizing oppression was a diversification of the energy needed in correcting the present situation of oppression. The black church was too adaptive to oppression, and it relegated liberation to an eschatological orientation that caused the black church to conform rather than transform the present situation. Douglass saw that the black church "valued strong lungs rather than higher learning"[5] in its ministers. The reason Douglass would not join the ministers in praising God for the overthrow of slavery was due to his humanistic self-reliance. Douglass believed in the ultimacy of human beings in correcting economic, social, and political injustice. Anything outside the human realm could not be relied upon without human involvement. For Douglass, the black church had not done the necessary theological reconstruction that would free them from the stronghold of their psychological enslavement. Many of the ideas that the black church held about God were distorted and unrealistic in many respects. Douglass viewed the church and its ideas of God in the same vein as Benjamin Mays later observed:

> The Negro's social philosophy and his idea of God go hand in hand.... Certain theological ideas enable Negroes to endure hardship, suffer pain and withstand

---

[4] Philip S. Foner, ed., *The Life and Writings of Frederick Douglass*, vol. 5 (New York: International Publishers, 1975) 47.

[5] Frederick Douglass, *The Life and Times of Frederick Douglass* (New York: Macmillan Publishing Company, 1962) 285.

malad-justment, but...do not necessarily motivate them to strive to eliminate the source of the ills they suffer.

Since this world is considered a place of temporary abode, many of the Negro masses have been inclined to do little or nothing to improve their status here; they have been encouraged to rely on a just God to make amends in heaven for all the wrongs they have suffered on earth.... Believing this about God, the Negro...has stood back and suffered much without bitterness, without striking back, and without trying aggressively to realize to the full his needs in the world.[6]

Lost in this otherworldly or eschatological view of a better world, the oppressed neutralize any idea that promotes confrontation with oppressive structural institutions. Political encounters and social and economic challenges are discouraged due to the feeling of trepidation that things may get worst or that these activities are going against God's design and purpose. Believing all things are in the hands of God, the oppressed portray themselves as being totally helpless, and they view God as an almighty bellhop who is summoned to do for the oppressed what they choose not to do for themselves. There is no wonder Douglass refused to join the ministers in thanking God for the overthrow of slavery. He felt they had not done enough for social reform and had not been delivered from the priest-craft and superstition that had caused a counterrevolutionary spirit, stifling social reform. Douglass understood that in order for a people to free themselves, they must first be freed from the conceptual system that controls their thinking. In a similar vein, Chinweizu later made the same observation:

---

[6] Benjamin E. Mays, *The Negro's God* (New York: Atheneum, 1969) 155.

The central objective in decolonizing the African mind is to overthrow the authority which alien traditions exercise over the African. This demands the dismantling of white supremacist beliefs, and the structures which uphold them, in every area of African life.... Economic and political control can never be complete or effective without mental control. To control a people's culture is to control their tools of self-definition in relationship to others.[7]

Until a reconstruction and decodification of the values that served to maintain oppression occurred, Douglass was reluctant to accept the black church as an autonomous, viable institution that would uplift the downtrodden. Gayraud Wilmore, the author of *Black Religion and Black Radicalism*, which is the most important textbook on the history of black religion and the black church could not understand why Douglass rejected the idea of a black church given what he saw in the white church against black people.

It is difficult to understand how Frederick Douglass, who rejected the idea of a black church, could have persuaded himself—given what he saw of the Presbyterians and Episcopalians—that the white churches of the North were ready to accept blacks on a basis of equality. The situation that existed in the Methodist Church when Allen and Jones withdrew continued to exist in many white churches into the twentieth century. Even after segregated seating was abolished in the North, blacks continued to be discriminated against in many subtle ways, such as being passed over for pastoral visitation and elective

---

[7] Cited from Naim Akbar, *Know Thy Self* (Tallahassee, Florida: Mind Productions & Associates, 1998) ii.

offices and being excluded from the more fashionable and intimate functions of the society-conscious city congregations.[8]

Wilmore failed to take into account Douglass's integrationist posture and the maintenance needs of oppression. Douglass fought for inclusion in the American democracy of freedom and justice. He rejected any idea of blacks leaving the land in which they were central in cultivating. Douglass wanted the same rights, privileges, and protection under the law as any other American citizen. He stated, "I expect to see the colored people of this country enjoying the same freedom, voting at the same ballot-box,...going to the same schools, attending the same churches, traveling the same street cars, in the same railroads cars,...proud of the same country, fighting the same foe, and enjoying the same peace, and all its advantages."[9] In spite of the legacy of slavery, too much had been invested to separate.

Additionally, Douglass knew firsthand that the black church was heavily influenced by the slave theology of the South, a theology that focused on the kind of theism that promoted quietism in the face of white oppression. Because the religion of the oppressed "is merely a loan from the whites who have enslaved and segregated the Negroes;...and is dominated by the thought of the oppressors of the race,...the Negro church often fulfills a mission to the contrary of that for which it was established."[10] Douglass understood the maintenance needs of oppression, and he saw that the black church had not

---

[8] Gayraud S. Wilmore, *Black Religion and Black Radicalism*, 2d ed. (New York: Orbis Book, 1983) 253.

[9] Cited from James H. Cone, *Martin & Malcolm & America* (New York: Orbis Books, 1991) 6.

[10] Carter G. Woodson, *Miseducation of the Negro* (Washington, D.C.: Associated Publishers, Inc., 1933, 1969) 68.

made a paradigm shift from the racist/sexist worldview of their oppressors and had not reached the point of removing God's overruling sovereignty from human history and replacing it with human sovereignty over human history; therefore, he rejected the idea of a black church. Until the black church was willing to put its energies into eliminating oppression in its many forms, Douglass was unwilling to accept the black church as an authentic liberating institution. He viewed the black church with the same lens as E. Franklin Frazier:

> The Negro church with its own forms of religious worship was a world which the white man did not invade but regarded with an attitude of condescending amusement. The Negro church could enjoy this freedom so long as it offered no threat to the white man's dominance in both economic and social relations. And, on the whole, the Negro's church was not a threat to white domination and aided the Negro to become accommodated to an inferior status. The religion of the Negro continued to be otherworldly in its outlook, dismissing the privations and sufferings and injustices of this world as temporary and transient.[11]

One can see why Douglass had his misgivings about the black church. He could not in all good conscience postpone a God-given right to liberty and justice to some future eschatology. Douglass's focus was on the present reality in order to show his oppressed people that freedom and equality were radical possibilities within human history. The transformation of the social, economic, and political spheres of

---

[11] E. Franklin Frazier, *The Negro Church in America* (New York: Schocken Book, 1974) 51.

earthly history was not a matter of fulfillment beyond this life, but a present reality of a new age. But as long as the oppressed procrastinated and focused on a future relief from a present misery, the future age would be just as dim as the present.

To give vision and direction toward liberation, the black church desperately needed trained ministers. Douglass knew that if there were any trained ministers, they were few in number. His desire to see an integrated church was due to his hope that blacks would be exposed to a kind of theological education that would correct their misreligion and discourage compliance to the status quo. Douglass's thirst for the liberation of the oppressed was buttressed by the Anti-Slavery Society, which he considered the true church. From Douglass's perspective, the black church as an autonomous institution had not proven itself to be a liberating institution. This is not to imply that the white church was any better. But those whites and blacks who were members of the Anti-Slavery Society came closer to being the true church than what Douglass had previous seen in the organized churches of the North and South.

Furthermore, Douglass knew that the black church and many of its ministers were too dependent upon God's intrusion in human affairs. Many of them stood back and prayed for God to do for them what they could actually do for themselves. Douglass rejected the idea of God's intrusion from without, focusing instead on human activity from within. Douglass and many black ministers could not see eye-to-eye on God's all-powerfulness and human powerlessness. When the Civil War was over and there was a celebration for the recent ratification of the Fifteenth Amendment to the Constitution, black ministers criticized Douglass for not thanking God for this change. From Douglass's perspective, the overthrow of slavery would not have happened had it not been for the brave men and women who labored to destroy it. Giving thanks to these brave soldiers for being instruments of social reform was the only way Douglass could "get a glimpse of God anywhere." Human activity made the difference, not the escapist prayers and praises of the clergy, who professed to love God but failed to devote their lives to the liberation of the oppressed. Black ministers condemned slavery and oppression, but they did not take action. The "denunciation [of an evil system] is impossible without a commitment to transform, and there is no transformation without action."[12] Douglass said, "One honest Abolitionist was a greater terror to slaveholders than whole acres of camp-meeting preachers shouting glory to God."[13]

According to Douglass, giving thanks to God for human deeds is wrong because it makes God responsible for the crimes of human history. Such thanks "assumes that the heavenly father is always with the strong, against the weak, and with the victors against the vanquished,"[14] that is, that God favors the white race over the black race, the male over the female, a view that makes God into a malevolent deity, depending on who is the conquered or dominated group. And "'if God chose a side and stood for anything at all,' Douglass reasoned, 'He sided with and stood for the immutability and efficacy of the moral law, regardless of human sophistry.' 'A finite creature,' Douglass concluded, 'has no right to discriminate between the acts of an infinite God.'"[15]

---

[12] Paulo Freire, *Pedagogy of the Oppressed* (New York: Continuum Publishing Company,1993) 68.

[13] Foner, ed., *The Life and Writings of Frederick Douglass*, 5:50.

[14] *The Frederick Douglass Papers*, "It Moves," Washington: Library of Congress, 1976 (Manuscript Division, Microfilm 28:18).

[15] Waldo E. Martin, *The Mind of Frederick Douglass* (North Carolina: University of North Carolina Press, 1984) 182.

Douglass could do without the religious platitudes of the clergy and welcome more their service to uplift the downtrodden. When Bishop Campbell, the leading black clergy of Philadelphia, pushed the issue further about Douglass's refusal to thank God, Douglass replied,

> If Bishop Campbell...in place of getting up these church meeting to try to distant heretics like myself, would honestly go to work and endeavor to reform the character, manners, and habits of the festering thousands of colored people who live in the utmost misery and destitution in the immediate vicinity of Big Bethel, he would do more to prove his church sound than by passing any number of worthy resolutions about thanking God. It was always more common to meet with men who would profess love to God whom they have not seen than to show love to man whom they have seen.[16]

In order to heal the oppressed masses, Douglass rejected giving them more religion. In fact, as we have stated earlier, Douglass believed the reason slavery existed was because of too much religion. The more religious America became, the less humane it seemed. He also surmised that it was the misreligion of the oppressed that caused them to work at cross-purposes with their liberation. When religion is used to seek salvation outside instead of inside human history, oppressed people will not develop a revolutionary practice to transform their condition. What the oppressed needed was not more religion, but an adequate understanding of oppression and its operations

---

[16] Philip S. Foner, ed., *The Life and Writings of Frederick Douglass*, vol. 4 (New York: International Publishers, 1975) 50.

and disguises in order to reduce if not eliminate it all together. In his appeal to the philanthropists who sought to build churches in the black communities, Douglass stated, "It is something to give the Negro religion. It is more to give him justice. It is something to give him the Bible, it is more to give him the ballot. It is something to tell him that there is a place for him in the Christian's heaven, it is more to let him have a place in this Christian country to live in peace."[17]

Notwithstanding the criticism of the black clergy and their traditional religious beliefs, another thing that furthered alienated the clergy from Douglass was his stand for the equal rights of women. As an advocate of human liberation, Douglass fought no less for women's liberation than he did for black liberation. The same argument that justified the inferiority and enslavement of blacks was used to keep women oppressed and disenfranchised. Douglass knew that the liberation of women would require the same persistent agitation and organization as black liberation. Women had been a part of Douglass's life from start to finish. A group of British antislavery women purchased his freedom. They raised funds that enabled Douglass to purchase a printing press to establish his own publication, *The North Star*. When financial problems forced Douglass to suspend publications, the women came to his rescue.[18] As Douglass saw it, blacks' and women's liberation were intertwined, and he was "willing to be part of the bridge over which women should march to the full enjoyment of their rights."[19]

---

[17] Herbert Aptheker, "An Unpublished Frederick Douglass Letter," *Journal of the Negro History* 44 (July 1959): 279.

[18] Philip S. Foner, *Frederick Douglass on Women's Rights* (New York: Da Capo Press, 1992) 10.

[19] Ibid., 39.

Douglass was the only man found in the circle of women's rights conventions. He was far ahead of his contemporaries in understanding oppression and its effects on people, regardless of their race or gender. From the inception of his first publication, *The North Star* carried the slogan, "Right is of no sex." Douglass understood that sexism and racism were twin evils, one no less ominous than the other. Douglass saw the abolition of sexism as an integral part of the human rights struggle as the abolition of racism. Rejecting traditional religious beliefs that supported male supremacy, Douglass accented that the struggle for women's rights "is the cause of human brotherhood as well as the cause of human sisterhood, and both must rise and fall together. Woman cannot be elevated without elevating man, and man cannot be depressed without depressing woman also."[20]

Therefore, as part of common human equality and unity, Douglass said, "The rights of woman and the rights of man are identical—we ask no rights, we advocate no rights for ourselves, which we would not ask and advocate for woman."[21] What is good and wholesome for man is equally the same for woman. If the moral law of the universe is violated when men are deprived of their human rights, it is equally violated when women are deprived of theirs. Human rights granted to one part of the human family and denied to the other part of the human family work at cross-purposes with the wholeness of a new humanity. For Douglass, the liberation struggle to free men and not women was inauthentic. Douglass said, "This woman suffrage movement is but a continuance of the old anti-slavery movement. We have the same sources of opposition to

---

[20] "The Ladies," *North Star*, 10 August 1848, in Foner, *Frederick Douglass on Women's Rights*, 49; Address Before Woman Suffrage Convention, n.d., in Foner, *Frederick Douglass on Women's Rights*, 125.

[21] "The Rights of Woman," *North Star*, 28 July 1848, 50.

content with, and we must meet them with the same spirit and determination, and with much the same arguments."[22]

Douglass saw no moral distinction between the struggles against racism and sexism. Both are equally part of the oppressive structures of society that require equal attention, dedication, and intelligence for their removal. Though there is no moral distinction between the two evils, Douglass conceded that women's liberation was a much greater cause because to liberate women would be to liberate and elevate half of the whole human family. Those who suffered the greatest in this male-dominated world were the women and children, and Douglass recognized this in his social analysis. He stated,

> Victor Hugo has said many true and touching things of the miseries of man, but he has never said anything truer or more touching than this: "He who has seen the misery of man only has seen nothing: he must see the misery of woman: He who has seen the misery of woman only has seen nothing: he must see the misery of children." To man there are a thousand ways to escape to one for woman.[23]

Though women were oppressed the most in the world's society, Douglass knew that he could not speak for women as women could speak for themselves:

> I believe no man, however gifted with thought and speech, can voice the wrongs and present the demands of women with the skill and effect, with the power and authority of woman herself. The man struck is the man to cry out. Woman knows and feels her wrongs as man

---

[22] Frederick Douglass to Oliver Johnson, 1885, in Foner, ed., *The Life and Writings of Frederick Douglass*, 4:427; "Emancipation of Women," 28 May 1888, in Foner, *Frederick Douglass on Women's Rights*, 118.

[23] Foner, *Frederick Douglass on Women's Rights*, 135.

cannot know and feel them, and she also knows as well as he can know, what measures are needed to redress them. I grant all the claims at this point. She is her own best representative. We can neither speak for her, nor vote for her, nor act for her, nor be responsible for her; and the thing for men to do in the premises is just to get out of her way and give her the fullest opportunity to exercise all the powers inherent in her individual personality, and allow her to do it as inherent in her individual personality, and allow her to do it as herself shall elect to exercise them. Her right to be and do is as full, complete and perfect as the right of any man on earth. I say of her, as I say of the colored people. Give her fair play, and hands off.[24]

Many arguments based upon religion and nature were raised against women's equality with men. These arguments were used to continue the oppression of women and the refusal of the church and the government to advocate the cause of women's liberation. Douglass challenged those who were in opposition with the Woman's Rights movement:

If any man can give one reason, drawn from the nature and constitution of man, why he should have a voice in the selection of those who shape the policy and make the Laws of the Government under which he lives, which reason does not apply equally and as forcibly to woman, I for one, shall like to hear that reason. To me, the sun in the heavens at noonday is not more visible than is the right of woman, equally with man, to participate in all that concerns human welfare, whether in the Family, in Reform Associations,

---

[24] Ibid., 110.

Educational Institutions, in the Church or in the State. Until this Right is admitted, secured, and exercised, count me among the friends of the Woman's Right's Movement.[25]

Douglass knew as a whole that women were marginalized. He also knew that there were particular problems facing black women. Black women had to contend with not only being women, but with being black. Douglass stated the difference between black and white women:

> When women because they are women, are dragged from their houses and hung upon lamp-posts; When their children are torn from their arms, and their brains dashed upon the pavements; when they are objects of insult and outrage at every turn; when they are in danger of having burnt down over their heads; when their children are not allowed to enter schools; then they have an urgency to obtain the ballot equal to our own. [When someone in the audience shouted, "Is that not all true about black women?"] Douglass replied: Yes, yes, yes; it is true of the black woman, but not because she is a woman, but because she is black.[26]

Though the difference between black women and white women was clear to Douglass, he fought to enfranchise all women. Women both black and white impressed Douglass on every level during the antislavery movement. Observing their commitment to the cause of human liberation, Douglass said that this "caused me to be denominated a woman's-rights man." He further acknowledged the work "of the honorable women, who have not only assisted me, but who according to

---

[25] Ibid., 78.
[26] Ibid., 32–33.

their opportunity and ability, have generously contributed to the abolition of slavery, and the recognition of the equal manhood of the colored race."[27] To deprive women would be to deprive the world of love, peace, character, intelligence, etc.—things that held this world together over against the heartless and destructive nature of men. Douglass stated,

> The heart of woman is ever warm, tenderly alive, and throbs in deepest sympathy with the sorrows and sufferings of every class, color, and clime, over the globe. She is the last to inflict injury and the first to repair it. If she is ever found in the ranks of the enemies of freedom, she is there at the bidding of man, and in open disobedience to her own noble nature.[28]

Douglass saw the best of humanity represented in women. As a liberation visionary, siding with the oppressed women for their liberation was a moral duty. When no one else pleaded the cause of women's equality and justice, Douglass stood firm with the oppressed women. When others neglected to give women their recognition in the struggle for human liberation, Douglass did not fail to recognize them. He could not overlook their contributions to human emancipation. In a letter to Harriet Tubman, Douglass honored her for her superior labors in the struggle against inhumanity:

> I have had the applause of the crowd and the satisfaction that comes of being approved by the multitude, while the most that you have done has been witnessed by a few trembling, scarred, and foot-sore bondmen and women, whom you have led out of the house of bondage, and whose heartfelt "God bless you"

---

[27] Douglass, *The Life and Times of Frederick Douglass*, 472.
[28] Ibid., 470.

has been your only reward. The midnight sky and the silent stars have been the witnesses of your devotion to freedom and your heroism. Excepting John Brown—of sacred memory—I know of no one who was willingly encountered more perils and hardships to serve our enslaved people than you have. Much that you have done would seem improbable to those who do not know you as I know you. It is to me a great pleasure and a great privilege to bear testimony to your character and your works, and to say to those to whom you may come, that I regard you in every way trustful and trustworthy.[29]

When Ida B. Wells worked to influence Congress to pass an anti-lynching law and encountered opposition in her quest to stop the inhumanity against the oppressed, Douglass recognized her contributions to the liberation struggle:

Brave woman! You have done your people and mine a service which can neither be weighed nor measured. If American conscience were only half alive, if the American church and clergy were only half christianized, if American moral responsibility were not hardened by persistent infliction of outrage and crime against colored people, a scream of horror, shame and indignation would rise to Heaven wherever your pamphlet shall be read.[30]

---

[29] Foner, *Frederick Douglass on Women's Rights*, 159.
[30] Ibid., 162.

There was never an opportunity in which Douglass did not recognize the contributions of women in the human rights struggle. In many of his speeches and articles and in his three autobiographies, Douglass included a tribute to women.[31] One biographer wrote, "Douglass' feminism, like his abolitionism, signified a struggle to foster human emancipation as a means toward human understanding and unity. A profound belief in human equality clearly undergirded these lofty and laudable aims."[32] Recognizing the invaluable work and commitment of women in the struggle for human liberation, Douglass stated,

When the true history of the Anti-Slavery cause shall be written, women will occupy a large space in its pages; for the cause of the slave has been peculiarly woman's cause. Her heart and conscience have supplied in large degree its motive and mainspring. Her skill, industry, patience, and perseverance have been wonderfully manifest in every trial hour. Not only did her feet run on "willing errands," and her fingers do the work, which in large degree supplied the sinews of war, but her deep moral convictions, and her tender humane sensibilities, found convincing...expression by her pen and her voice.[33]

It is clear from the foregoing analysis that Douglass was developing key patterns of thought of liberation theology. In the process of developing his theological perspective, Douglass had to painstakingly examine the theological tradition of Christianity that was being practiced in America. He found it flawed and polluted in many respects. There were beliefs and

---

[31] Ibid., 40.

[32] Martin, *The Mind of Frederick Douglass*, 138.

[33] Douglass, *The Life and Times of Frederick Douglass*, 469.

values that stifled the movement toward liberation. But that which worked at cross-purposes with liberation, Douglass dumped in order to keep in line with the ever-present demands of the gospel, a call for deliverance from the economic, social, and political structures of oppression.

Convinced that the true gospel was a liberating one, Douglass was a constant burning rebuke to the religious and political establishment of the status quo. His whole life was devoted to the release and uplift of the downtrodden. In whatever else he may have failed, Douglass did not fail in being "an unflinching, unflagging and uncompromising advocate and defender of the oppressed. When [slaves] were slaves [Douglass] demanded their emancipation, and when [they] were free, [Douglass] demanded their perfect freedom—all the safeguards of freedom."[34] For fifty-seven years, Douglass fought to enlighten the oppressed so they may loose themselves from the theological and philosophical beliefs that riveted their slavery and oppression more firmly. More importantly, once we understand Douglass's evolution as a move toward the development of a liberation theology, we will understand what he had to abandon in order to develop a theological perspective that was compatible with liberation from oppression.

In February 1895, after returning home from a meeting of the National Council of Women in Washington, D.C., Douglass died of a sudden heart attack. Headlines around the country carried the news. A once obscure slave had risen to the status of a national symbol. The news of Douglass's death spread like wildfire. Numerous editorials pointed out Douglass's contributions to the betterment of humanity and the nation as a whole. Elizabeth Stanton's letter shows the loss that many felt at the passing of this great man:

---

[34] Foner, ed., *The Life and Writings of Frederick Douglass*, 4:113.

He was the only man I ever saw who understood the degradation of the disenfranchisement of women. Through all the long years of our struggle he has been a familiar figure on our platform with always an inspiring word to say. In the very first convention, he helped me to carry the resolution I had penned demanding woman suffrage. Frederick Douglass is not dead. His grand character will long be an object lesson in our National history. His lofty sentiments of liberty, justice, and equality, echoed on every platform over our broad land, must influence and inspire many coming generations.[35]

Paul Lawrence Dunbar, the famous black poet, remembered Douglass in *Lyrics of Lowly Life*:

He was no soft-tongued apologist;
He spoke straightforward, fearlessly uncowed;
The sunlight of his truth dispelled the mist.
And set in bold relief each dark-hue cloud;
To sin and crime he gave their proper hue.
And hurled at evil what was evil's due
The place and cause that first aroused his might
Still proved its power until his latest day.
In Freedom's lists and for the aid of Right
Still in the foremost rank he waged the fray;
Wrong lived; his occupation was not gone.
He died in action with his armor on![36]

---

[35] Foner, *Frederick Douglass on Women's Rights*, 41.
[36] Paul Lawrence Dunbar, "Frederick Douglass," *Lyrics of Lowly Life* (New York: Dodd, Mead and Company, 1897) 8–11.

Frederick Douglass is a towing figure in American history. His influence and tenacity for justice and equality for all people cannot go unforgotten. It is the author's hope that those who analyze the life of Frederick Douglass will agree that he was working on a theological perspective that would give rise to the now-known liberation theology—a theology that is not an otherworldly escape from the hard realities of this world, but one that arises within these realities, empowering the oppressed to become active participants in their own economic, social, and political liberation.

4

DOUGLASS AND THE MAKING OF A LIBERATION THEOLOGY

Liberation theology was not formed in a vacuum. It came forth as a longing over the years for oppressed people to have meaning in the midst of being treated meaninglessly. The indignities that the oppressed suffered through the misuse of the Christian religion as practiced in America left them with no hope or frame of reference that would release their reality as human beings. The theological consciousness of the oppressor was so deeply imbedded in the American culture that every move toward "setting the captives free" was met with harsh resistance by many whites. But Douglass knew he had to recover the meaning of the gospel of Jesus Christ if there was to be a bursting forth of a fuller humanity for the oppressed. In this chapter we shall see two themes that Douglass lifted up and how the two themes have influenced other thinkers in the formulation of a liberation theology. The two themes are the point of departure for theological discourse and the cooperation between God and humanity for social reform.

The gospel of Jesus Christ for a fuller humanity was so deeply covered by layers of racism, sexism, and sectarianism that it proved to be a Herculean task for Douglass to uncover its oppressive packaging and convince the nation to chart another course. Nevertheless, Douglass resolved to "set the captives free" from economic, social, political, and religious oppression.

To break the chains of oppression, Douglass had to first break the psychodynamics of racism that held him in bondage. He stated, "For a long time when I was a slave, I was led to think from hearing such passages as 'servants obey your masters' that if I dared to escape, the wrath of God would follow me."[1] Douglass knew that the oppressed were defined by the theological and anthropological idiosyncrasies of white racism, and he was determined to define himself and help free the oppressed from their false consciousness. Once the oppressed free themselves from false consciousness, then they can counter the racist presuppositions and stratification necessary for their liberation. Douglass refused to be labeled by racism and to accept any interpretation that made him docile in his condition. Reading and reflecting on the gospel of Jesus Christ in a context of oppression, Douglass believed that the "Great Redeemer," Jesus the Christ, placed himself on the side of the poor and the oppressed; whosoever does likewise is at the heart of true Christianity.

In July 1859 Douglass wrote about his understanding of Christ's religion and its particular tilt. The religion of Christ "was for [humanity],…and for the poor [person], especially and particularly for the poor [person].… The religion of Jesus is

---

[1] *National Anti-Slavery Standard*, 28 October 1847.

like himself, a copy of himself. His heart is with the bleeding heart of humanity."[2]

To assist in the deliverance of the oppressed, Douglass armed himself with the religion of Jesus Christ. Whatever purpose religion serves, its core purpose should be the removal of hardships and wrongs, which oppressed people suffer continuously. If religion does not serve to remove the reality of racism and its manifestation in economic, social, and political realms, then it is not the religion of Christ but of the oppressor. Douglass recognized the "widest possible difference—so wide, that to receive the one as good, pure, and holy, is of necessary to reject the other as bad, corrupt, and wicked. To be the friend of the one is of necessity to be the enemy of the other."[3]

Douglass understood Jesus' statement that "you cannot serve two masters. You must love one and hate the other." Allegiance must be given to one and total rejection to the other. The oppressed must reject the ideological or cultural hegemony in the matrix of domination. They must go through a process of deconstruction and reconstruction to refute institutional mechanisms that are used to point out their subservient place in the world and create a space for themselves with the education, ideas, beliefs, and values that would enhance and maintain their total liberation. In this process, Douglass saw how religion was a main factor in the enslavement of his people. He was grieved that the church, which was supposed to represent the good, pure, and holy, was a bed partner with the bad, corrupt, and wicked. The church was serving the maintenance needs of oppression by converting religion into a tool to legitimate oppression.

---

[2] *Douglass' Monthly*, July 1859.
[3] Frederick Douglass, *Narrative of the Life of Frederick Douglass: An American Slave* (New York: Penguin/Book, 1982) 118.

Douglass characterized those who endorsed slavery and oppression as "rotten religionists" who neglected the oppressed, the fatherless, and the widow. Ten thousand times over Douglass preferred the gospel of Jesus Christ, which beat with the heart of the oppressed and injured, rather than the gospel of "miserable trash," which many evangelical Christians were advocating. The evangelical Christians were more concerned about "forms and ceremonies," revivals and "temple worship," while doing nothing for the suffering and injured slaves. When the evangelical Christians would go to the Bible seeking support for slavery, Douglass would point out in the same Bible the contrary. Douglass stated,

> The [person] that will go to God, or to the Bible, to look for arguments in support of a desire to work [another person] without wages, is a hypocrite as well as a scoundrel, and is below the level of argument. Some things are to evidently wrong to admit of argument or apology. Humanity instinctively turns from slavery with a shudder. We have here the utterance of the voice of God in [humanity], and to its high and instantaneous teaching we may listen in preference to any voice for slavery drawn from the Bible.[4]

Douglass was equally critical of the evangelical Christians who were advancing an eschatological salvation. Douglass refuted this nebulous afterlife. He wanted freedom "not only from physical chains but [from] the chains of superstition—those which not only galled the limbs and tore the flesh—but those which marred and wounded the human

---

[4] *Douglass' Monthly*, March 1861.

soul."[5] Douglass asserted that the gospel of Jesus Christ is not a postponement of justice and the release of the captives for an eschatological salvation. The gospel of Jesus Christ speaks of salvation in terms of a present reality, and Douglass would not accept any religion or interpretation "that despises [his] humanity in this world while it promises [him] a place in heaven."[6] There are needs on earth that cannot be met by waiting for salvation outside of human history. Douglass stated that "when a child first comes into the world, it don't cry for metaphysics or for theology, but for a little milk."[7] If a child does not receive the milk it cries for, then eschatological milk cannot save the child in this world. The child dies and the shame is on those who could have prevented the child's death. Douglass held the church in utter shame for allowing the slaves and the injured to die when the church held the power to help prevent it.

It was Douglass's belief that the gospel of Jesus Christ was a demand for economic, social, and political milk. To get this milk would require struggle and conflict and the reconceptualization of the gospel of Jesus Christ, helping the oppressed receive the milk that the evangelical Christians were withholding from them. Douglass wanted the oppressed to understand that the milk of justice could not be achieved by prayer alone. It would necessitate "a martyr-like spirit of self-sacrifice, and the firm reliance on Him who has declared Himself to be 'the God of the oppressed.'"[8]

---

[5] Frederick Douglass, *The Life and Times of Frederick Douglass* (New York: Pathway Press, 1941) 588–89.

[6] Frederick Douglass to Mr. Deane, 21 November 1890, Douglass Papers, Library of Congress.

[7] *Baltimore Sun*, 7 September 1891.

[8] Philip S. Foner, ed., *The Life and Writings of Frederick Douglass*, vol. 2 (New York: International Publishers, 1950 - 1975) 140.

Here we see the contour of Douglass's early theological development. Douglass believed God takes the side of the oppressed to bring them out of their oppression. But Douglass firmly believed that the liberation of the oppressed would come only with their participation. He believed that "when anything is to be done in this world some denizen of this world has got to do it, or it will go undone."[9] The oppressed could not sit back and wait for God to do for them what they needed to do for themselves.

At a 19 May 1870 celebration in Baltimore, Douglass stated, "I loved everything of Maryland except slavery—it was that I ran away from thirty-two years ago.... I found that God never began to hear my prayer for liberty until I began to run. Then you ought to have seen the dust rise behind me in answer to prayer."[10] Douglass believed it superstitious to think that God would do everything for the oppressed: "It is idle, a hollow mockery, for us to pray to God to break the oppressor's power, while we neglect the means of knowledge which will give us the ability to break this power."[11] David Howard Pitney stated, "By the 1850s, Douglass was a thoroughgoing religious liberal, or humanist. His liberal Protestantism coexisted comfortably with Enlightenment ideals of natural law and reason. Douglass's humanistic worldview was anchored in both Christian theology and natural rights philosophy, and his experience with religion helped form and support his humanistic faith."[12] What Howard-Pitney calls humanism, I will argue later in this chapter is a different form of humanism, namely, what William R. Jones calls humanocentric theism.

---

[9] *New Era*, 14 July 1870.

[10] Ibid., 26 May 1870.

[11] *North Star*, 14 July 1848.

[12] David Howard-Pitney, "Frederick Douglass: Abolitionist and Political Leader," in *African-American Humanism: An Anthology*, edited by Norm R. Allen Jr. (New York: Prometheus Books, 1991) 22.

To understand Douglass's view of God in the liberation struggle and why he moved from a God-centered stance to a human-centered stance, stressing the power and ultimacy of humankind, it is necessary that we compare and contrast traditional concepts of God and what is advanced by a liberation theology. We shall treat the concept of God and the different positions of liberation theologians who have a theological concern for theism, but who stand at opposite poles of the theological spectrum in the struggle for liberation. On one side of the theological pole is the position of theocentric-Christocentric theism, which depends upon God through Christ to liberate the oppressed. The opposite side of the theological spectrum is that of humanocentric theism, which depends upon humans to liberate themselves. Douglass's position was more akin to the latter. His humanistic worldview influenced other subsequent thinkers to explore, interpret, and develop a theology of liberation.

In his own way, Douglass was trying to answer the question that Dietrich Bonhoeffer later raised: "How can we proclaim God in a world come of age?" In one way or another we all struggle with this open-ended question. It is open-ended because there is still no conclusive answer about God's activity in the world. Like Douglass, we are still trying to unravel the mysteries surrounding the relation of God to the finite causal nexus in nature and history. What is so difficult to do, without opting for either deism or atheism, is to proclaim God's intrinsic goodness and justice in a world that is torn by hate, greed, poverty, and oppression. Though we struggle to understand, our presuppositions about God are conflicting. They often create an antithesis that pushes us to different sides of the theological spectrum. The two incompatible realities of an all-powerful, loving God and an all-pervasive evil beg the question of God's sovereignty over human history and his involvement within human history. These contrasts and contradictions must be analyzed with more care so a more accurate conclusion can be drawn about how divine activity is involved, if at all, in human history. Douglass believed that divine activity came only through human beings because there was no evidence that it acted apart from humans themselves.

The concept of God is difficult and complex, but in the traditional classical view, God is viewed as omnipotent and utterly transcendent to finite human beings; nevertheless, God directs and controls every event. In contemporary thought, liberals view God as the "Sovereign Ground of Hope" who identifies with the weak and suffering people of the world. Liberals are compassionate but passive toward evil. Liberationists take action to end evil. They echo God's partiality to the poor and oppressed, making them the object of God's liberation. God will liberate the poor and the oppressed as God did in biblical history. God, having freed Israel from Egypt, is the same God who acted on behalf of blacks suffering from white oppression and on behalf of women suffering from patriarchal oppression. But just how God will act or is acting on behalf of the poor and oppressed is not clear, and this is a challenge and often a theological impasse for liberation theologians, as it was earlier for Douglass.

Still, the problem that liberation theologians cannot circumvent is the theodicy question. Since God liberated the oppressed from oppression in biblical history, why has God not acted on behalf of the oppressed today? Why are the oppressed still oppressed? These are serious questions that theologians cannot evade or drown in the tradition of dogmatism. For centuries the oppressed have put their deliverance in the hands of a God who has not yet delivered as God is said to have done in biblical history. There is no evidence of any "exaltation-liberation event" for the oppressed, and Douglass advised the oppressed not to look for such an event. With no evidence of an "exaltation-liberation event," the oppressed still postulate a God who distributes justice by rewarding the faithful and punishing the sinners. God, for them, is on their side, though the evidence points to the contrary, and the oppressed find themselves saying with W. E. B. Du Bois,

> O Silent God, though Whose voice afar in mist and mystery hath left our ears a hungered in these fearful days. Bewildered we are...mad with madness of a mobbed and mocked and murdered people; straining at the armposts of Thy Throne, we raise our shackled hands by the tears of our dead mothers, by the blood of Thy crucified Christ: What meaneth this? Tell us the Plan; give us the Sign! Sit no longer blind, Lord God, deaf to our prayer and dumb to our dumb suffering. Surely Thou too art not white, O Lord, a pale, bloodless heartless thing?[13]

Bishop Daniel Payne was also bewildered about God in the face of human suffering and oppression. In agony, Payne said,

> I began to question the existence of the Almighty, and to say, if indeed there is a God, does he deal justly? Is he a just God? Is he a holy Being? If so, why does he permit a handful of dying men to oppress us?... Thus I began to question the Divine government, and to murmur at the administration of his providence. And could I do otherwise, while slavery's cruelties were pressing and grinding my soul in the dust, and robbing

---

[13] W. E. B. DuBois, "A Litany at Atlanta," in *Black Voices*, ed. Abraham Chapman (New York: New American Library, 1968), 372–73.

me and my people of these privileges, which it was hugging to its breast, and giving thousands to perpetuate the blessing which was tearing away from us.[14]

Nathaniel Paul was no less perplexed than DuBois and Payne when he questioned God's muteness during human misery:

Tell me, ye mighty waters, why did ye sustain the ponderous load of misery? Or speak, ye winds, and say why it was that ye executed your office to waft them onward to the still more dismal state; and ye proud waves, why did you refuse to lend your aid and to have overwhelmed them our billows?... And, oh thou immaculate God, be not angry with us, while we come into this thy sanctuary, and make the bold inquiry in this thy holy temple, why it was that thou didst look on with calm indifference of an unconcerned spectator, when thy holy law was violated, thy divine authority despised and a portion of thine own creatures reduced to a state of mere vassalage and misery.[15]

Clearly, we can see the absurdity of postulating a God who is thought to be unlimited in power and goodness, but who has not demonstrated it in the life of the oppressed for their liberation. Why lay claim to such a God? Douglass believed that the answer is found within the belief and value system of

---

[14] Cited in James H. Cone, God of the Oppressed (Minnesota: The Seabury Press, Inc., 1975) 188.

[15] Nathaniel Paul, "An Address Delivered on the Celebration of the Abolition of Slavery in the State of New York, July 5, 1827," in Carter G. Woodson, Negro Orators and Their Orations (New York: Russell and Russell, 1969) 69.

the oppressed, that is, the idea and unceasing hope that God will free them from oppression in God's own good time. This belief and value system was what Douglass worked hard to change among the oppressed. The oppressed believed that God's providential care for his people may be frustrated for a time by the powers of evil, but God's justice, in the final analysis, will deliver the oppressed from oppression. And when God gets ready to move on behalf of the oppressed, oppressive structures can no longer stand in the way.

Critics of this belief system, such as Carter G. Woodson, Benjamin Mays, and William R. Jones, agree with Douglass that such a belief commits the fallacy of begging the question, that is, of assuming as true what is to be proved. They also point out with convincing structural validity that such a belief about God has promoted the miseducation and misreligion of the oppressed. It has served as a major curtailment of the corrective activity needed to gain liberation and has fostered a laissez-faire attitude in the revolutionary struggle.

Douglass, Woodson, Mays, and Jones have shown how belief regulates action and how the oppressed are responsible for their continued suffering and oppression. They contend that the beliefs and values of the oppressed have so bound them that they show no resistance to their oppression because they believe their predicament is somehow in the plan of God. Douglass vehemently rejected this notion, and Mays later wrote about how the oppressed are contained:

> If death comes to you, it comes because God permits it, and if God permits it, you ought to take a Christian view of the situation. If God permits it to come to you, just say, "I am no better than anybody else." We ought not to set ourselves against God and say God has not done justice by us. The implication here seems to be that God permits everything to

happen that does happen and there is nothing man can do about it. Things could not happen if God did not permit them to happen. That belief...goes a long way in helping people to adjust themselves to the inevitable. However painful and heart-rending the death of mother may be, the load is perhaps easier to carry if that person believes that it was God's will. Even though the idea may be false, it has great value for the person who believes it.[16]

Mays continues with his analysis by pointing out how the beliefs of the oppressed about God help them psychologically by providing them hope and assurance that God is on their side; since they live in this world of injustice with which they cannot cope, they leap to another world more akin to their fancy. At the same time Mays points out how this nullifies the spirit of rebellion needed to bring about economic, social, and political reform. As Douglass discovered how the oppressed were caught in the "power of superstition and priest-craft," in a similar vein Mays later discovered the same thing:

The Negro's social philosophy and his idea of God go hand in hand.... Certain theological ideas enable Negroes to endure hardship, suffer pain and withstand maladjustment, but...do not necessarily motivate them to strive to eliminate the source of the ills they suffer.

Since this world is considered a place of temporary abode, many of the Negro masses have been inclined to do little or nothing to improve their status here; they have been encouraged to rely on a just God to make amends in heaven for all the wrongs they have suffered

---

[16] Benjamin E. Mays, *The Negro's God* (New York: Atheneum, 1969) 71–72.

on earth. In reality, the idea has persisted that hard times are indicative of the fact that the Negro is God's chosen vessel and that God is disciplining him for the express purpose of bringing him out victoriously and triumphantly in the end. The idea has also persisted that "[the] harder the cross, the brighter the crown." Believing this about God, the Negro…has stood back and suffered much without bitterness, without striking back, and without trying aggressively to realize to the full his needs in the world.[16]

These beliefs about God may be psychologically satisfying, but they are, as Mays sees it, "highly compensatory and counterrevolutionary." Oppression maintains itself by convincing the oppressed that "the Lord disciplines [those] whom he loves, and chastises every [child] whom he receives. It is for discipline that you have to endure. God is treating you as [children]; for what [child] is there whom his father does not discipline? If you are left without discipline, in which all have participated, then you are illegitimate children and not sons [and daughters]" (Hebrews 12:6-8 RSV). The crux of this belief is that suffering and oppression are God's chastisement, and as long as the oppressed buy into such a belief, the chances are nil that they are going to fight their oppression. Unless there is a renewing of the mind of the oppressed, they will continue to view suffering as positive and to take it as synonymous with being children of God. For them, heaven is a place that will reward them for enduring suffering and oppression on earth.

Emil Brunner's position is also representative of the same compensatory analysis just described. He asserts "what…ought to be," which closes off every avenue of reform that needs to take place if liberation is to become a reality. This type of

---

[16] Ibid., 155.

affirmation as normative leads inevitably to quietism and a reconciling of the sufferers to their suffering, and it makes God a malevolent deity who is playing games with humanity. It means that humans have no volition that God will respect; God will overrule humans' wills in order to achieve divine purpose. Based on Brunner's position, oppression must be in the will and divine plan of God, though Brunner worked hard in his *Divine Imperative and Social Justice* to avoid this conclusion. Thus, Brunner writes, "All that is, and all that happens, takes place within the knowledge and the will of God.... All that happens is connected with the divine purpose; all is ordered in accordance with, and in subordination to, the divine plan and the final divine purpose."[17]

The problem with Brunner's position is that God is held responsible for the crimes of human history, an idea Douglass refuted in his analysis. It was Douglass's belief that the foundation of oppression was built not by God, but upon the pride, power, and avarice of humans. God is not responsible for the crimes of human history. But Brunner postulates the position that God is the creator of evil as well as the good. Whatever evil is inflicted upon humans, including the slaughter of innocent children, is, according to Brunner, in God's will. Indeed Brunner must embrace this conclusion if he is not to contradict his system of divine sovereignty.

A. N. Whitehead makes a similar argument to Brunner's. He states that God is "the supreme author of the play, and to Him must therefore be ascribed its shortcomings as well as its success."[18] God must be held responsible for the good as well as the evil that takes place on the stage of human history. Humans

---

[17] Emil Brunner, *The Christian Doctrine of Creation and Redemption* (Philadelphia: Westminster Press, 1952) 155.

[18] Alfred North Whitehead, *Science and the Modern World* (New York: The MacMillan Company, 1931) 258.

cannot be held responsible because they are not the supreme author of events, nor can they determine the outcomes. Brunner's and Whitehead's conception of God is bipolar. God is good as well as evil, and whatever happens in life, good or evil, must be predestined by God or work into G.W. Leibniz's "preestablished harmony...which evil may serve toward a greater good.... The 'best of all possible world's' is possible precisely because of the evils as well as the goods which have gone into its becoming."[19]

In a similar vein with Douglass, James Cone rejects Brunner's, Whitehead's, and Leibniz's position because it would mean that Hitler was God's instrument in the slaughter of six million Jews and the Europeans were God's instrument during the Middle Passage when tens of millions of Africans lost their lives. What is inferred is that the "best of all possible worlds" would not be possible if evil was not included. Attacking this absurdity, Cone writes,

> Black theology rejects the tendency of classical Christianity to appeal to divine providence. To suggest that black suffering is consistent with the knowledge and will of God and that in the end everything will happen for the good of those who love God is unacceptable to black people. The eschatological promise of heaven is insufficient to account for the earthly pain of black suffering.[20]

Though liberation theologians agree that compensatory beliefs about God and the idea of evil as divine purpose must

---

[19] Marjorie Hewitt Suchocki, *Process Eschatology in Historical Context: The End of Evil* (New York: State University of New York Press, 1988) 21.

[20] James H. Cone, *A Black Theology of Liberation* (New York: Lippincott, 1970, 1986) 44.

be discarded by the oppressed if liberation is to become a reality, they find the inquiry into just how God is acting on behalf of those who are suffering and oppressed to be problematic. The claim that God is good, just, and a liberator must be supported by empirical evidence. If there is no evidence, then the claim collapses. Rudolf Bultmann tried to bridge this gulf:

> The only way to preserve the unworldly, transcendental character of the divine activity is to regard it not as an interference in worldly happenings, but something accomplished in them in such a way that the closed weft of history as it presents itself to objective observation is left undisturbed. To every other eye than the eye of faith the action of God is hidden. Only the "natural happening" is generally visible and ascertainable. In it is accomplished the hidden act of God.[21]

Bultmann's theory may be very attractive for some, but to others, like William R. Jones, the theory does not solve the problem of divine malevolence. Jones said, "When one makes conclusions about Who God is on the basis of what He has done for [the oppressed].... We should not presuppose God's 'intrinsic goodness for all of mankind but let this conclusion emerge, if at all, on the basis of His actual benevolent acts in behalf of all."[22] Jones asserts that God must speak for himself and not be expected to be a projection of the presupposition of those in power. God is only accessible in the act of justice on behalf of the oppressed today.

---

[21] Cited from Owen C. Thomas, ed. *God's Activity In the World: The Contemporary Problem* (California: Scholars Press, 1983) 56.

[22] William R. Jones, *Is God a White Racist?* (New York: DoubleDay Anchor, 1973) 14.

Like Jones, Langdon Gilkey also sees the shortcomings of making conclusions about God from the past that may not square with his relation to the world today. It is obvious that the world is still full of evil, suffering, and oppression, and to make conclusions about God without the evidence creates an empty void that makes our analogies of God's mighty acts nothing less than wishful thinking. Thus, Gilkey writes,

> What we desperately need is a theological ontology that will put intelligible and credible meanings into our analogical categories of divine deeds and of divine self-manifestation through events.... Only an ontology of events specifying what God's relation to ordinary events is like, and thus what his relation to special events might be, could fill the now empty analogy of mighty acts, void since the denial of the miraculous.[23]

Unlike Nietzsche and William Hamilton, who advocate the "death of God" theology, Jones contends that traditional Christian theism cannot be reconciled to the claim of divine benevolence in light of human suffering, especially human suffering that is occasioned by racism. Jones is in serious dialogue with his colleagues about the type of model projected for treating the suffering of the oppressed. He cautions his colleagues about the risk of theological collapse caused by putting liberation into the hands of a God who has yet to prove his credibility. To advocate the ultimacy of God constitutes a theodicy problem; it begs the question of God's benevolence for some and his malevolence for others. To avoid implicating God as being malevolent toward the oppressed by virtue of their condition, Jones accents another form of theism,

---

[23] Langdon Gilkey, "Cosmology, Ontology, and the Travail of Biblical Language," *Journal of Religion* 41:200, 203 (1961).

humanocentric theism, which ultimately makes humans responsible for the crimes of human history and liberation. To advocate the ultimacy of God begs the question of malevolence and credibility.

James Cone asserts that God is credible through Jesus Christ. What God has done through Christ makes God not only credible, but the true liberator of the oppressed. Cone states that "Christianity begins and ends with the man Jesus—his life, death, and resurrection. He is the Revelation, the special disclosure of God to man, revealing who God is and what his purpose for man is. In short, Christ is the essence of Christianity."[24] Cone believes that Christ is the decisive event of liberation, and the resurrection is the victory over sin, death, and oppression. And though suffering is still with us and "is wrong,...it has been overcome in Jesus Christ."[25] Through him, God has shown his love for us and that he has sided with the oppressed for their liberation, and they have been made free to fight along with God in the struggle. The liberating act of God is clearly in the resurrection of Jesus Christ. Thus, Cone asserts,

> As he delivered the Israelites from Egypt, he will also deliver black people from white oppression.... On the cross, God encounters evil and suffering, the principalities and the powers that hold people in captivity; and the resurrection is the sign that these powers have been decisively defeated, even though they are still very active in the world. But the victory in Jesus' resurrection is God's liberating act.... We have

---

[24] James H. Cone, *God of the Oppressed* (Minnesota: Seabury Press, 1975) 268.

[25] Ibid., 192.

been given the gift of freedom to fight with God in the liberation struggle.[26]

On the other hand, William Jones believes that the crucifixion is not necessarily a sign of God's love for humanity; it could be interpreted as divine malevolence against humanity. We must admit that this historical event is certainly paradoxical, in the sense that God's love for humanity is demonstrated by divine hostility. But whatever position we embrace, Jones believes that the suffering of Christ as a symbol of God's salvation for humanity plays a major part in helping the oppressed to reconcile to their suffering:

> By arguing that human suffering should be endured and accepted because God Himself has suffered even more, the strategy is laid to keep man, particularly the oppressed, docile and reconciled to his suffering. Accordingly, human suffering does not become a springboard to rebellion. The one act that will initiate man's ultimate deliverance and humanization, the one act that will dignify man is nipped in the bud—precluded, as it were, by God's supreme act of love! God's act in Christ, then, becomes not an act for man's highest good, but against it. And the principle that we should love God because He first loved us collapses.[27]

The essential point Jones is making is that there is a fine line between God's favor or disfavor, God's grace or God's curse. Any form of human suffering can be interpreted as God's hostility. What could be thought of as divine salvation could as easily be divine damnation. Since "suffering is multi-evidential," we cannot draw any correct conclusive

---

[26] Ibid., 236.
[27] Jones, *Is God A White Racist?*, 8.

interpretation of suffering based on suffering itself. Therefore, Jones is calling for a reconstruction of the theological framework of the Judeo-Christian tradition, which projects a God who continuously performs deliberate acts in and through human history. Without successfully refuting the charge of divine prejudice and racism, the respective system of this type of theism would lead to blaming God for the crimes and suffering of human history. This is incompatible with the claim of God's intrinsic goodness and benevolence toward mankind.

What Jones wants us to come to grips with, without begging the question of the maldistribution of ethnic suffering, is that God is not responsible for the crimes of human history; humans are responsible, and they are also responsible for their own liberation. This is the position that Douglass postulated later in his life. Douglass advised his oppressed people not to look for miracles. Jones advises us that without advocating the functional ultimacy of humans, we automatically implicate God as a "white racist."

Thus, Jones breaks away from the old patterns of thought, as Douglass did before him, and moves into another intellectual realm in which the familiar arguments that God will liberate the oppressed can be dismissed as irrelevant. Jones cuts deeply at the traditional theological and philosophical presuppositions of theologians who rest their case on the foundation that God will save us from the ravaging effects of economic, social, and political oppression. Jones believes we must save ourselves and draw upon our responsible efforts because humans are not so absolutely depraved that they can do nothing but wait on God. Therefore, Jones rejects Cone's theocentric and Christocentric theism and asserts what he calls humanocentric theism as the most appropriate vehicle for treating the suffering of the oppressed. Jones believes that replacing this type of theism for the one described by Cone and others will better situate God in relation to human efforts in their history and destiny.

Humanocentric theism claims the cosmic freedom and autonomy of humanity. It is grounded in the anthropological functional ultimacy of humankind, rather than the ontological superiority of the Transcendent. Humanocentric theism eliminates the allegation of divine racism and elevates humans to areas of control "that previous theological traditions reserved for God alone."[28] To transfer areas of control to humans is to affirm their authentic created freedom. William Daniel Cobb said, "God created [humans] with the intention that [humans] should make what God did not make and...that [humans] make what God did not think to make as a consequence of God's gracious self-limitation of his own power in the act of creating [humans]." To affirm the ultimacy of humans is to give humans "space in which to be more than a robot or a puppet in a stage play."[29]

According to the humanocentric theist, God respects the freedom of humans, and God will not violate the law under which he made humans. Eliezer Berkovits says,

> [Humans] alone can create value: God is value. But if [humans] alone [are] the creator of values...then [they] must have freedom of choice and freedom of decision. And [their] freedom must be respected by God himself. God cannot as a rule intervene whenever [humans'] use of freedom displeases him.... If there [are] to be [humans], [they] must be allowed to make [human] choices in freedom.[30]

---

[28] Ibid., 187.

[29] William Daniel Cobb, "Morality in the Making: A New Look at Some Old Foundations," January 1-8 Century, 11.

[30] Eliezer Berkovits, *Faith After the Holocaust* (New York: KTAV Publishing House, 1973) 105.

For God to intervene in human history at points of displeasure is to collapse the argument of human free will and action. And, as Epictetus would say, "No one can rob us of our free will."[31] John Milton makes the same claim in *Paradise Lost* that God by nature made us free mortal agents: "Good he made thee, but to persevere. / He left it in thy power, ordained thy will / By nature free, not over-ruled by Fate / Inextricable, or strict necessity."[32]

What Douglass and others have said is that freedom is God's will, and God does not interfere in the affairs of humanity when the affairs are grievous to God. God is not the instigator that causes particular things to happen. As Kenneth Cauthen of Colgate Divinity School has said, "It is not even proper to say that God permits them, since events are produced by autonomous causes in nature or by autonomous choices of human beings."[33] Since events are produced by humans, then God is vindicated. What has happened in human history has been the result of the conscious decisions and choices of human beings. This is why Douglass, Jones, and others have moved away from Cone's theocentric and Christocentric theism, which argues for God's controlling influence and sovereignty over the human situation.

The consequence of Jones's humanocentric theism "is to remove God from anyone's side. History becomes open-ended and multivalued, capable of supporting either oppression or liberation, racism or brotherhood."[34] He further explains his position:

---

[31] John A. O'Brien, *Truths Men Live By* (New York: The MacMillan Company, 1946) 248.

[32] Ibid, 248.

[33] A Kenneth Cauthen lecture at Colgate Rochester Divinity School (Rochester, New York) October 1989.

[34] Jones, *Is God A White Racist?*, 196.

The desacralization of politics delivers political affairs from divine hands, as once thought, and into human hands. We move, as it were, from the politics of God to the politics of [humans]. And the consequence of the deconsecration of values is to "place the responsibility for the forging of political systems, in man's own hands." Thus the functional ultimacy of man relative to value and history is affirmed.[35]

Though this theistic framework of Jones has a secular flavor that places him outside the mainstream of American religion, especially the black religion, his position cannot be dismissed. We must face the inconsistencies that are so prevalent in the opposite theological position of theocentric theism. Even James Cone admits that "theologians ought to be grateful to William Jones for having brought this problem to our attention so sharply…. Christian theologians have to admit that their logic is not the same as other forms of rational discourse."[36] What Jones's position shows is that black religion is not monolithic, as was demonstrated in the life of Douglass.

Inasmuch as Jones's position is considered razor sharp, other religious thinkers and philosophers of the past and present share Jones's humanocentric view. Not only did Douglass share this view during the horrible days of slavery, but other African Americans asserted features of humanocentric theism in the struggle for freedom. Robert Alexander Young, who issued a manifesto in defense of slaves' rights, exalted the slaves' activity, rather than divine activity, as a consequence of God's will for humankind. Young placed the responsibility for freedom squarely on the shoulders of blacks themselves. He believed that God in his power had decreed of

---

[35] Ibid., 190–91.
[36] Cone, *God of the Oppressed*, 188, 191.

the human person "that either in himself he stands, or by himself he falls."[37] Thus, Young wrote to the slave owners this militant message:

> Weigh well these my words in the balance of your conscientious reason, and abide the judgment thereof to your own standing, for we tell you of a surety, the decree hath already passed the judgment seat of an undeviating God, wherein he hath said, "surely hath the cries of the black, a most persecuted people, ascended to my throne and craved my mercy; now, behold! I will stretch forth mine hand and gather them to the palm, that they become unto me a people, and I unto them their God."[38]

In other words, Young asserted that God's hands were the hands of the slaves; they would be the ones to bring God's judgment upon the slaveholders, calling for a revolution until freedom was attained.

It is not certain that David Walker read Young's manifesto, but Walker also believed that slaves had to take upon themselves the task of breaking the chains of slavery. Whatever action was necessary to free themselves from slavery, they would have to perform it. To do so would be to answer the call of God. In his appeal, Walker said,

> If you commence, make sure [your] work—do not trifle, for they will not trifle with you—they want us for their slaves, and think nothing of murdering us in order to subject us to that wretched condition—therefore, if

---

[37] Gayraud S. Wilmore, *Black Religion and Black Radicalism*, 2d ed. (Maryknoll NY: Orbis Book, 1983) 36.
[38] Ibid.

there is an attempt made by us, kill or be killed.... Look upon your mother, wife and children, and answer God Almighty! And believe this, that it is no more harm for you to kill a man, who is trying to kill you, than it is for you to take a drink of water when thirsty;—in fact, the man who will stand still and let another murder him, is worse than an infidel, and, if he has common sense, ought not to be pitied.[39]

This appeal of Walker is unambiguous. He took the responsibility of human freedom out of God's hand and placed it squarely in the hands of the oppressed. The oppressed were the ones who controlled their situation and destiny. Walker is made it a sin to pity any person who stood by and let another person murder him because he felt that God would intervene on his behalf—Walker felt this inaction was worse than being an infidel.

Obviously there were other blacks, along with Douglass, in the nineteenth century who asserted features of humanocentric theism in their religious thought. Others include Gabriel Prosser, Nat Turner, and Denmark Vesey. Though these men have not been given high commemoration in the black church, they nevertheless were willing to work alone with God as a "codetermining power" relative to the accomplishment of God's will on earth as it is in heaven.

Jewish philosopher Martin Buber believes that since God made humans, God created a spot so that humans can share in his sovereignty, at least over the human situation. Insomuch as God is creator, humans have the freedom to be co-creators. God made humans and gave them dominion over all the earth, which means that they must take charge over the human situation and destiny. As free co-creators, Buber states,

---

[39] Ibid., 42.

Man can choose God and he can reject God.... That man has the power to lead the world to perdition implies that he has power to lead the world to redemption.... These two powers of man constitute the actual admission of man into mightiness.... The fact remains that the creation of this being, man, means that God has made room for a codetermining power, for a starting-point for events.... Does that mean that God cannot redeem the world without man's help? It means that God wills not that He could do that. Has God need of man for His work? He wills to have need of man.... Does this mean that God has given away one particle of His power to determine the course of events? We only ask that question when we are busy subsuming God under our logical categories. In the moment when He breaks through we have an immediate experience of our freedom, and yet in these moments we also know by an immediate experience that God's hand has carried us.[40]

Buber argues, as Douglass did, for the participation of humans if liberation is to be a reality. God did not create humans to be mere spectators, but to be involved participants in making this world a better place in which to live. God is not going to drop out of the sky and shape the future for humans; humans have the responsibility of doing this themselves. Harvey Cox makes the same argument by stating that humans are the steersmen of the future. He sees humans as "that point where the cosmos begins to think and steer itself."[41] This is to say that the misery of our present time is a constant companion

[40] Cited in Jones, *Is God A White Racist?*, 187–88.
[41] Cited in Frederick Herzog, *Liberation Theology: Liberation in Light of the Fourth Gospel* (New York: Seabury Press, 1972) 9.

until we as humans decide to abolish it. Howard Burkle asserts that God acts as a persuader, not a dictator: "God communicates, solicits, and tries by rational means to affect our choices. We are always responding to influences, which are encouraging us to think, weigh and choose. Whenever [humans] seize the possibilities of freedom and acts from within [their] own being, [they] are certifying the persuasive activity of God."[42] Gutierrez says since humans are "the center of creation, it is integrated in the history which is being built by [human] efforts."[43]

What Douglass and these religious thinkers point out so clearly is that our biggest problem in this world is ourselves. We are the irresponsible ones when it comes to economic, social, and political reform. As Frederick Herzog states,

> God is not our problem. We are our problem. As long as we tend to make God our "problem"...we tend to run away from ourselves and turn into oppressors and exploiters. God, if he be God, can take care of himself. His becoming concrete in the visible Word is not so much for straightening out our problem with God as for sensitizing us to who we are.[44]

In the final analysis, whatever our presuppositions of God may be, and however neatly packaged our religious systems are in debating or disclaiming God in the liberation struggle, "what stands out in liberation theology is not the action of God, but that of man. What [a liberation theologian] hopes for is a world 'fashioned by [man's] own hands'; not so much a theophany, or manifestation of God, as an 'anthropophany,' or

---

[42] Howard Burkle, *The Non-Existence of God* (New York: Herder & Herder, 1969) 207.

[43] Cited in Emilio Nunez C., *Liberation Theology*, translated by Paul E. Sywulka (Chicago: Moody Press, 1985) 185.

[44] Frederick Herzog, *Liberation Theology*, 35.

manifestation of man."[45] We can see from the foregoing analysis why Douglass made the functional ultimacy of humans the determiner of human values and history, rather than the ontological superiority of the Transcendent. He believed it was in human hands to break the chains of slavery and oppression in order to accomplish economic, social, and political liberation. Making humans the determiner of human values and history is not robbery or rebellion against God and his ultimacy, but an affirmation of human freedom. Douglass's analysis on subsequent freedom fighters has made room for a strand of thinking, though outside of the black traditional mainstream, to form a theology that would not only motivate the oppressed to act on their own behalf, but also help to develop black intellectualism that would aid the cause of freedom and justice in the world.

Just how much influence Douglass has had on the formulation of a liberation theology cannot be measured. But anybody who is serious about liberating the oppressed, especially using a black theology of liberation as a tool, cannot undervalue the influence Douglass has had in shaping such a theology. Though it was not until the late 1960s that the idea of a black theology of liberation surfaced as a theological reflection by those involved in the liberation struggle, Douglass's deconstruction and reconstruction of ideas and theology were already on record. James Cone and others took the experience of blacks in America and linked this with the established interpretation of the gospel, and "in so doing Cone opened up the possibility of a black theology of liberation that was neither Protestant nor Catholic, but the way black

[45] Cited in Emilo Nunez, *Liberation Theology*, translated by Paul E. Sywalka (Chicago: Moody Press, 1985) 205.

Christians think, feel, and act about their liberation with the intensity of an ultimate concern."[46]

William B. McClain pointed out the importance of black theology:

> "New occasions teach new duties," James Russell Lowell observed long ago. New history also demands new theological construction. It was this truth that black theology discovered and has led us into new ways of approaching our theological task. It departed from the Euro-American way of theological reflection. It moved us from a theology of orthodoxy to a theology of ortho-praxis. It became clear to black theological thinkers that our ethics had outrun our theologies. What black theology said was that the church could no longer engage in what Paul Tillich called the "denial of justice in the name of holiness."[47]

The creators of black theology linked the liberation struggle with the gospel of Jesus Christ, thus mixing religion and politics together. This linking of religion and politics together was viewed as out of the norm by a great majority of white churches and theologians who thought that the two should be kept in splendid isolation. This is the same reason Douglass broke with the Garrisonians. Douglass saw the need to wed the two, and he knew that if the struggle produced any gains those gains had to be secured by legislation. Therefore, in the twentieth century the political process had to be linked to the social disruptions that were taking place in the 1950s and

---

[46] Wilmore, Black *Religion and Black Radicalism*, 218.

[47] William B. McClain, *Black People in the Methodist Church* (Nashville: Abingdon Press, 1984).

1960s to bring about change in the American society for the oppressed. James Cone put it this way:

> Black Power and black religion are inseparable. Both seek to free black people from white racism. It is impossible for Black Power to be effective without taking into consideration man's religious nature. It is impossible for black religion to be truly related to the condition of black people and to the message of Jesus Christ without emphasizing the basic tenets of Black Power. Therefore, Black Theology seeks to make black religion a religion of Black Power.[48]

Looking back over history and seeing a reoccurring theme of political and social liberation, figures like Frederick Douglass put their own spin on interpreting what the Christian faith means in a context of oppression. They knew that white religion did not reflect the life and teaching of Jesus Christ. If it did, black people never would have been pillaged and enslaved by religious justification. Therefore, Douglass and those he influenced knew that they needed a theology that would speak to their struggle for liberation. They no longer wanted to be defined by the theological and anthropological idiosyncrasies of white racism. Their frame of reference had to be different from that of their oppressors; they had to see life from their own particular context in order to release their reality. Therefore, liberation theology became the byproduct of a long struggle of oppressed people to find meaning and freedom in a world that denied it to them.

In order to understand the impact Douglass's thought has had upon the formulation of a liberation theology, it is

---

[48] James H. Cone, *Black Theology & Black Power*[(Maryknoll NY: Orbis Books, 1997) 130.

necessary first to understand the prerequisites of a liberation theology. This involves identifying liberation theology's specific purpose and method. The purpose identifies its objective, and the method is the means for reaching that objective, and the means is dictated by the "sitz in leben," or the sociological context. Descriptions of these core concepts will enhance the understanding of liberation theology and its legitimacy as a Christian theology.

First and foremost, liberation theology's specific purpose is to bring about the economic, social, and political liberation demanded in the Bible. As far back as Isaiah, we find the demand for justice that is accented in liberation theologies. God is speaking to his prophet concerning the needs of the poor and the oppressed. Indicting an oppressive society and demanding justice, the prophet made the following charges:

> What to me is the multitude of your sacrifices? Says the LORD; I have had enough of burnt offering of rams, and the fat of fed beast; I do not delight in the blood of bulls, or of lambs, or of he goats. When you come to appear before me, who requires of you this trampling of my courts? Bring no more vain offering; incense is an abomination to me; New moon and Sabbath and the calling of the assemblies—I cannot endure iniquity and solemn assembly. Your new moons and your appointed feasts my soul hates; they have become a burden to me, I am weary of bearing them. When you spread forth your hands, I will hide my eyes from you; even though you make many prayers, I will not listen; your hands are full of blood. Wash yourselves; make yourselves clean; remove the evil of your doing from before my eyes; cease to do evil, learn to do good; *seek justice, correct oppression; defend the*

fatherless, plead for the widow (Isaiah 1:11-17, emphasis added, RSV).

The purpose, then, of a liberation theology is to get rid of injustice in a world where so many of God's people are victimized every day. Gustavo Gutiérrez says that this purpose is "a theological reflection born...of shared efforts to abolish the current unjust situation and to build a different society, freer and more humane."[49] Until our energies are directed toward putting an end to unjust situations, our religion and its forms of worship are not acceptable to God.

The second purpose of liberation theology is to develop the orthodoxy and orthopraxy for the first purpose. Such a development will not only affect the way the gospel has been previously proclaimed, but also the way in which theology is done. In other words, liberation theology legitimates its goal of overcoming unjust situations by showing through the Scriptures that economic, social, and political injustice is not only a violation of human rights, but also an insult to God. To fight against oppression is the will of God, and the Christian church is called to take action against injustice in order to free the oppressed from their oppression.

Gutierrez illuminates this understanding by stating that liberation theology is not just an academic pursuit; it "does not stop with reflecting on the world, but rather tries to be part of the process through which the world is transformed."[50] He further states the theological undertaking:

> The theology of liberation attempts to reflect on the experience and meaning of the faith based on the commitment to abolish injustice and to build a new

---

[49] Gustavo Gutierrez, *A Theology of Liberation* (Maryknoll NY: Orbis Books, 1973) ix.

[50] Ibid., 15.

society; this theology must be verified by the practiced of that commitment, by active, effective participation in the struggle which the exploited classes have undertaken against their oppressors. Liberation from every form of exploitation, the possibility of a more human and more dignified life, the creation of a new [person]—all pass through this struggle.[51]

The struggle to transform the social reality of the oppressed does not take place apart from struggling communities, but it is precisely within the oppressed communities that we come to understand God's self-revelation in history and liberation theology's point of departure for theological discourse and social action.

The criticism that Douglass and Cone have of Western theology and its point of departure is that the cultural elite's theological framework was structured toward maintaining the present unjust situation. Western theology has been mainly partisan, in the sense that it did not take into account the wretchedness of the oppressed. In fact, much of Western theology aided and abetted the defense of the rich and powerful sociopolitical position, especially the religious leaders who merely became priests to the status quo and sanctifiers of the powers that be.

For example, when the peasants in medieval Europe (1524–1525) protested against the economic and social disabilities under which they suffered, Martin Luther, the chief pioneer of Protestantism, sided with the state in putting down the revolt. His course of action was buttressed by what he perceived the role of the church to be in society. Luther was mainly concerned about the church in its connection with the preaching of the word of God, which, enlivened by the Spirit,

---

[51] Ibid., 307.

governs human beings in matters pertaining to otherworldly salvation. One writer noted, "Luther's emphasis upon the Bible led him into deep sympathy with the Gospel ethic of love, which was utterly opposed to the ordinary life of the world, to the secular nature of the struggle for existence, to the lust of power, to law, and to the desire to amass possessions."[52] Yet Luther also believed that God assigned institutions of government to defend against tumult or anarchy, and though these institutions of government have flaws and defects, they do play a role in God's scheme of things, and by no means should these institutions be compelled into any kind of Christian conversion by force, but through the preaching of God's word the government may become a state. In the final analysis, Luther believed that the "church ought to exercise her influence [primarily] on spiritual lines."[53]

With this understanding of Luther's mindset, it is predictable that he would issue a pamphlet called "Against the Murderous and Thieving Hordes of Peasants," denouncing the actions of the peasants and advising the state to annihilate the oppressed for their rebellion against the state. The peasants' revolt fell outside of Luther's understanding of the roles of church and state. Of course, liberation theologians see Luther's position as too narrow in scope and, therefore, inadequate. Regardless of his mindset, his position supported the maintenance of the present situation, which meant that the oppressed should continue to be reconciled to the status quo without protesting their suffering. Because Luther did not champion the cause of the class from which he had sprung, the

---

[52] Ernst Troeltsch, *The Social Teaching of the Christian Churches*, vol. 2, translated by Olive Wyon (Louisville: Westminster/John Knox Press, 1992) 485.

[53] Ibid., 494.

peasants regarded him as traitor.[54] He fell short of the "praxis" needed to bring about economic, social, and political reform. George H. Williams says, "The peasants had been everywhere crushed because they had no universally recognized leader and only an improvised organization, and had to make do with the evangelical counsel of a few prophetic clerics and the military skills of a few disaffected knights."[55] This example of religious leaders siding with the rich and powerful is typical of the Western church and its theology, with only a few notable exceptions.

In America, the white church became the defender and guarantor of slavery and oppression. Kyle Haselden notes,

> So far as the major denominations are concerned, it is the story of indifference, vacillation, and duplicity.... It is a history in which the church not only compromised its ethic to the mood and practice of the times but was itself actively unethical, sanctioning the enslavement of human beings, producing the patterns of segregation, urging upon the oppressed Negro the extracted sedatives of the Gospel, and promulgating a doctrine of interracial morality which is itself immoral.[56]

More unfortunate still, the mainstream white church became the cultural guardian of domination, which helped to foster social annihilation, economic exploitation, and political suffocation of the poor and the oppressed. From the sixteenth century to the mid-nineteenth century, with the exception of

---

[54] Kenneth Scott Latourette, *A History of Christianity* (New York: Harper & Brothers Publishers, 1953) 725.

[55] George Huntston Williams, *The Radical Reformation* (Philadelphia: Westminster Press, 1972) 81.

[56] Kyle Haselden, *The Racial Problem in Christian Perspective* (New York: Harper & Row, 1959) 63.

some Quakers and a few other Christians, the white church never championed the cause of black people. While they were being "despised, insulted, ignored, whipped, cudgeled, hunted down by bloodhounds, seized by mobs and slashed and burned and hanged and blown to pieces," the white church generally remained mute and insensitive.[57] Even worse, white ministers and theologians by and large were more interested in law and order, which was really ordered injustice, than they were in economic, social, and political justice.

After the Civil War, white church interpretation of the gospel message was quiet on the subject of racial oppression. The gospel was preached in such a way that it became an integral part of a society that denied blacks the rights to human freedom. In the same vein as Frederick Douglass, James Cone said that white theologians never made the oppressed their theological point of departure; therefore, they "missed the decisive ingredient of the gospel message."[58] Their overall theological concern was "with the universal dimension in the gospel, which transcends the particularities of the Black experience. The particular concerns of Black people, they contended, were at best an ethical problem or even a pastoral problem and thus more appropriately belonged in the 'practical' department."[59] Concomitantly, from Jonathan Edwards to Walter Rauschenbusch and the social gospel movement—all neglected to see the problem of black oppression. America dismissed black suffering into invisibility, as Ralph Ellison would say, "simply because [white America]

---

[57] Fred D. Wentzel, *Epistle to White Christians* (Philadelphia: The Christian Education Press, 1948) 49.

[58] Cone, *God of the Oppressed*, 51.

[59] Gayraud S. Wilmore and James H. Cone, *Black Theology: A Documentary History, 1968–1979* (Maryknoll NY: Orbis Books, 1979) 136.

refuse to see [them]."[60] Refusing to see the oppressed caused their situation to worsen.

Not until the Civil Rights movement, which was led by a brilliant young minister by the name of Martin Luther King Jr., do we find America coming to grips again with black suffering. King took black suffering to the streets to show the world that America has not lived up to its promises of democracy and fair play. There was this inconsistency of being a leader of the free world and the maltreatment of black citizens. King created the kind of confrontation that called into question the image of America in the eyes of the world. Though America initially rejected King and the Civil Rights movement, the wheels of justice were turning too fast, and America was forced to make some adjustments in its social and political policies. The nonviolent struggle that King led did bring about changes in the social and political life of America, but when blacks started to echo "Black Power," it was a repudiation of the abuse of white power, which had victimized blacks for centuries. King rejected the slogan "Black Power," and so did many others in the Civil Rights struggle. After King was assassinated on 4 April 1968, many blacks wondered if further progress could be made through nonviolent means. They knew they needed a frame of reference rooted and grounded in the black experience but not bound by white, Western civilization.

Black theologians began to reflect on the life and message of Malcolm X, who was at the other end of the theological spectrum. Malcolm preached "by any means necessary," and he promoted Black Nationalism as a way to deal with the problem of White Nationalism. Under the present system, Malcolm believed there was no way blacks could win their liberation

---

[60] Ralph Ellison, *Invisible Man* (New York: Random House Publisher, 1947) 3.

because the rules of the game were created and controlled by white oppressors. The only way oppressed blacks could get anywhere in this country and the world was to make up their own rules:

> The time that we're living in…now is not an era where one who is oppressed is looking toward the oppressor to give him some system or form of logic or reason. What is logical to the oppressor isn't logical to the oppressed. And what is reason to the oppressor isn't reason to the oppressed. The [oppressed] people [in this world] are beginning to realize that what sounds reasonable to those who exploit us doesn't sound reasonable to us. There just has to be a new system of reason and logic devised by us who are at the bottom, if we want to get some results in this struggle. Archie Epps, ed., *The Speeches of Malcolm X at Harvard* (New York: Morrow Press, 1968) 133.

In a similar vein, Lerone Bennett Jr. makes the same admonition concerning the need for the oppressed to develop a new frame of reference and to decolonize their minds from the theological concepts, beliefs, and values that make it easy to submit to oppression:

> The overriding need for the moment is for [the oppressed] to think with [their] own mind. We cannot see now because our eyes are clouded by the concepts of white supremacy. We cannot think now because we have no intellectual instruments save those which were designed expressly to keep us from seeing. It is necessary for us to develop a new frame of reference, which transcends the limits of white concepts. White concepts have succeeded in making [oppressed] people feel inferior. White concepts have created the conditions that make it easy to dominate a people. The

initial step towards liberation is to abandon the partial
frame of reference of our oppressor and to create new
concepts which release our reality.[61]

The way to release the reality of black people would be
"an interpretation of historic black faith grounded in the
experience of suffering and struggle, but also in a realistic
appraisal of the depths of white racism and the possibilities of
the black consciousness and power."[62] Black theologians knew
that their theology had to reflect the needs of the great masses
of black people both inside and outside of the Christian
church. Their theology must be a theology of the people rather
than an academic theology that makes no connection with the
people. Gayraud Wilmore explains what the black theologians
were carving out in an effort to reflect being black in a white,
racist society:

> In step with King, black theologians attempt to do
> Christian theology from a Christian social action and
> ecumenical perspective. In step with Malcolm, they
> refuse to be domesticated or dominated by the norms of
> white Christianity. If black theology tends in one
> direction more than another, it perhaps leans today
> toward Malcolm rather than Martin. It desires to be
> Pan-African rather than Euro-American. It identifies
> more with a Marxist social analysis and the liberation
> theologies of the Third World than with American
> liberalism and the neo-orthodox theology of Reinhold
> Niebuhr, which emphasized the insufficiency of human
> striving with history.[63]

---

[61] Lerone Bennett Jr., *The Challenge of Blackness* (Chicago: Johnson
Publishing Company, 1972) 36.

[62] Wilmore, *Black Religion and Black Radicalism*, 211.

[63] Ibid., 234.

After much discussion and debate, in 1970, James Cone, the author of *A Black Liberation Theology*, became the Malcolm X-Bennett prescribed remedy. The suffering of the oppressed was his point of departure, and his book gave justification to blacks struggling against nonbeing in a context of oppression. Cone stated, "Theology can never be nonpartisan.... It is either identified with those who inflict oppression or with those who are its victims."[64] Frederick Douglass stated earlier, "My hands were no longer tied by my religion."[65] Cone's black theology of liberation was no longer tied by the white religious interpretation of the gospel, which left black people despised and degraded. It was the long-awaited point of reference that the oppressed people needed in order to affirm their humanity and release their reality. Wilmore said, "Such a theology is rooted in the resistance to slavery and racism by the historic black church, but it includes more than organized religion. It embraces also the attempt of black secular and non-Christian groups to express verbally and act out existentially the meaning and values of the black experience in America, Africa, and the Caribbean."[66] A black theology of liberation opened up a way for other people who found themselves in a context of oppression to do a liberation theology. Whatever else can be said about black liberation theology, it is certain that Frederick Douglass helped to lay the groundwork for this type of theology to emerge.

---

[64] Cone, *God of the Oppressed.*
[65] Douglass, *The Life and Times of Frederick Douglass*, 139.
[66] Wilmore, *Black Religion and Black Radicalism*, 218.

5

INTERPRETATION OF DOUGLASS AS A

LIBERATION THINKER

The goal in this chapter is to encourage Douglass scholars to rethink their positions on his philosophical and theological development. Certain conclusions drawn about Douglass's religious odyssey have been made clear, such as the nature and cause of his evolutionary shift in theology. We can now offer another paradigm, which can expand the debate and put Douglass's thought in a more appropriate context, namely, as a thinker who anticipated liberation theology.

First of all, the author of this study is in agreement with other Douglass scholars that there was an evolution in his thought and that traditional religious beliefs worked at cross-purposes with social reform. Traditional religious beliefs as set forth in the Bible have formed the core of much of African-American religious life and culture. Douglass moved away from traditional Christian beliefs because they became the defender and guarantor of certain presumptions governing the etiquettes between the oppressed and their oppressors. Traditional religious beliefs reinforced an imbalance of power by convincing the oppressed that power was inherently evil so the oppressors could continue to possess a surplus of power while the oppressed suffered from a deficit of power.

Furthermore, Douglass abandoned traditional Christian beliefs because the way in which Christianity was interpreted to the oppressed offered them no hope of freedom in this world. E. Franklin Frazier writes,

> Not only did Christianity fail to offer the Negro hope of freedom in this world, but the manner in which Christianity was communicated to him tended to degrade him. The Negro was taught that his enslavement was due to the fact that he had been cursed by God. His very color was the sign of the curse which he had received as a descendant of Ham. Parts of the Bible were carefully selected to prove that God had intended that the Negro should be servant of the white man and that he would always be a "hewer of wood and a drawer of water."[1]

This kind of misreligion of the oppressed led to particular ideas of God or Christian theism. As noted earlier, there is a link between theological beliefs and oppression, which Benjamin Mays has identified as "compensatory." Another example Mays gives shows the negative impact that compensatory beliefs have on social reform:

> Thousands of people, particularly Negroes, have seen the compensatory results of these ideas in their own communities. Long before I knew what it was all about, and since I learned to know, I heard the Pastor

---

[1] E. Franklin Frazier, *Black Bourgeoisie* (New York: Collier Books, 1965) 115.

of the church of my youth plead with the members of his congregation not to try to avenge the wrongs they suffered, but to take their burdens to the Lord in prayer. Especially did he do this when the racial situation was tense or when Negroes went to him for advice concerning some wrong inflicted upon them by their oppressors. During these troublesome days, the drowning of Pharaoh and his host in the Red Sea, the deliverance of Daniel from the Lion's Den, and the protection given the Hebrew children in the Fiery Furnace were all pictured in dramatic fashion to show that God in due time would take things in hand. Almost invariably after assuring them that God would fix things up, he ended his sermon by assuring them further that God would reward them in Heaven for their patience and long-suffering on earth. Members of the congregation screamed, shouted and thanked God. The pent up emotions denied normal expression in everyday life found an outlet. They felt relieved and uplifted. They had been baptized with the "Holy Ghost." They had their faith in God renewed and they could stand it until the second Sunday in the month when the experience of the previous second Sunday was duplicated. Being socially proscribed, economically impotent, and politically browbeaten, they sang, prayed, and shouted their troubles away. This idea of God had telling effects upon the Negroes in my home community. It kept them submissive, humble, and obedient. It enabled them to keep on keeping on. And it is still effective [today].[2]

---

[2] Cited in William R. Jones, "Theological Response to 'The Church and Urban Policy'" *Journal of the Society for Common Insights* 2 (1978): 51.

However, Albert J. Raboteau feels that traditional forms of Christian theism do not necessarily lead to acquiescence. To conclude that they do, he feels, would be inaccurate. He asserts that the slave religion had different effects on slaves, depending on their different circumstances.

> To conclude, however, that [slave] religion distracted slaves from concern with this life and dissuaded them from action in the present is to distort the full story and to simplify the complex role of religious motivation in human behavior. It does not always follow that belief in a future state of happiness leads to acceptance of suffering in this world. It does not follow necessarily that a hope in a future when all wrongs will be righted leads to acquiescence to injustice in the present. Religion had different effects on the motivation and identity of different slaves and even dissimilar effects on the same slave at different times and in different circumstances. To describe slave religion as merely otherworldly is inaccurate, for the slaves believed that God had acted, was acting, and would continue to act within human history and within their own particular history as a peculiar people just as long ago he had acted on behalf of another chosen people, biblical Israel.[3]

Raboteau's argument shows that the slave religion did have an impact on some slaves who rebelled against their masters, and this study acknowledges that there were exceptions. But the critical variable in Mays' compensatory analysis is not based upon the afterlife, which leads to acquiescence, but a set of beliefs and values that encourages the

---

[3] Albert J. Raboteau, *Slave Religion* (New York: Oxford University Press, 1978) 317–18.

maintenance of, rather than reformation of, the present situation. The majority of slaves accepted a set of beliefs that negated attitudes and actions necessary for liberation. Because of these beliefs and values, there was never in the United States a massive uprising against the slave system, such as there was in the Haitian revolution of 1791, which "drove the English, Spanish, and finally, the army of Napoleon into the sea."[4] It is predictable how oppressed people will respond to the present situation based on their religious beliefs. Douglass abandoned the enslaving beliefs that reconciled him to his oppression, advancing instead a more effective theological approach that would eliminate the source of his suffering.

James B. Hunt applies Mays' concept of compensatory beliefs to Douglass's religious evolution. Douglass, he affirms, moved away from traditional religious beliefs and practices because of their negative impact for social reform. The emotionalism that so often eclipses the rational and practical application for social reform stifles the movement toward liberation. Hunts asserts it was Douglass's reliance on practical ethics rather than dogmatic orthodoxy that moved Douglass toward a new liberalism, a liberalism that focused on the actions of others as the preeminent way to "get a glimpse of God anywhere":

> For Douglass, progress for blacks would come through a purely rational, humanistic religion void of the shouting and jumping. This position is understandable given Frederick's experience with the oppression of slave-holding Christians and the prejudices of some abolitionists. Douglass' liberal faith granted him the self-reliance that he so desperately

---

[4] Gayraud S. Wilmore, *Black Religion and Black Radicalism*, 2d ed. (Maryknoll NY: Orbis Book, 1983) 23.

sought in his desire for freedom, liberation and intellectual autonomy.[5]

Similarly, Benjamin Quarles argues that Douglass abandoned the traditional form of Christian theism because it did not provide an adequate foundation for social reform, in particular the traditional form of Christian theism that put too much emphasis on "otherworldliness." This emphasis on "pie in the sky" immobilizes one from protesting and changing the economic, social, and political wrongs one suffers and causes one to be reconciled to the human suffering that social reform attempts to alleviate. Douglass, Quarles asserts, criticized the clergy because they preached a gospel of escapism:

> Douglass held that too many clergymen preached a gospel of resignation, of passiveness, of being so pre-occupied with the city called heaven that they did not rebel against the status quo here below. To Douglass religion should have been an instrument for social reconstruction; instead it was largely, he felt, the chief stock in trade of a theologically-untrained and "folksy" clergy who used it as a device for making the underprivileged forget social reality by fixing his eyes on a distant land of milk and honey to be reached by prayerfully waiting for the chariot to swing low.[6]

In a similar posture, Philip S. Foner reinforces this interpretation of Douglass's this-worldly focus on religion and its objective to provide features of the good life before life ends. Douglass was not concerned about "shoes, milk, and honey over yonder," but he saw the need for shoes, milk, and

---

[5] James B. Hunt, "The Faith Journey of Frederick Douglass, 1818–1895." *Christian Scholar's Review* 15/3 (1986): 245.

[6] Benjamin Quarles, *Frederick Douglass* (Washington, D.C.: Associated Publishers, Inc., 1948) 295.

honey down here: "The glaring contrasts between wealth and poverty...deepened Douglass' belief that religion was best which best served the interests of the mass of the people on earth.... Douglass favored less religion and few rags, less piety and fewer poor, fewer churches and more pure air and sunshine for the poverty-stricken."[7]

With this understanding as background, we can see that the traditional religious beliefs Douglass moved away from were based upon the dysfunction of those beliefs for social reform. Also, one can see Douglass's emphasis upon a belief and value system, that is, the worldview of a people or person as critical to how one acts. One writer notes, "Plato declared that we act on the basis of what we believe to be true about the fundamental categories of theology and philosophy.... He further stated that if our beliefs are inaccurate or unsound, our actions invariably will be inauthentic."[8] This observation parallels Carter G. Woodson's assertion that the mechanism of oppression requires a very specific set of values and beliefs. The oppressed are oppressed because their minds are held captive by their oppressors:

> Taught the same economics, history, philosophy, literature and religion which have established the present code of morals, the Negro's mind has been brought under the control of the oppressor. The problem of holding the Negro down, therefore, is easily solved. When you control a man's thinking you do not have to worry about his actions. You do not have to tell him to stand here or go yonder. He will find his "proper place" and will stay in it. You do not need to

[7] Philip S. Foner, ed., *The Life and Writings of Frederick Douglass*, vol. 4 (New York: International Publishers, 1952) 126.

[8] Cited in William R. Jones, *Is God A White Racist?* (New York: Double Day Anchor, 1973) 40.

send him to the back door, he will cut one for his special benefit. His education makes it necessary.[9]

Woodson's concept of the miseducation of the oppressed includes also their misreligion as an instrument of oppression. Miseducation and misreligion have caused the oppressed to become "otherworldly-quietistic." They have been taught "what is ought to be," which predetermines that change is inappropriate and unnecessary. Once this teaching is embraced, the oppressed are not motivated to cancel their economic, social, and political oppression. If liberation is to become a reality, the misreligion of the oppressed must be dumped or discarded, and this principle is evident in Douglass's religious odyssey.

The foregoing analysis identifies the point of agreement among scholars that Douglass did abandon traditional religious beliefs, which is another way of saying he abandoned traditional forms of Christian theism. Not only did traditional Christian theism have a one-dimensional focus on the other world, but its basic content supported the notion of a passive acceptance of the present situation. Scholars agree that Douglass moved from this position of acceptance.

However, contrary to other scholars' analyses of Douglass's movement from Christian theism, David W. Blight analyzes Douglass's movement differently. Blight does stress Douglass's emphasis upon social reform, but he traces this reform to a form of Christian theism. Whereas other scholars make mention of the elevation of the human agent in human affairs and history, Blight argues that Douglass elevates not the human agent, but an apocalyptic God who intervenes in the affairs of mankind:

---

[9] Carter G. Woodson, *The Mis-Education of the Negro* (Washington, D.C.: Associated Publishers, Inc., 1933, 1969) xxxiii.

By the 1850's, his thought exhibited virtually all
the religious and secular tenets of millennialism:
eschatological symbolism, God's second coming and
retributive justice, and the American sense of mission as
a "redeemer nation."... Douglass garnered long-range
hope for the cause of black freedom from an apocalyptic
God who could enter history and force nations, like
individuals, to chart a new course.[10]

From Blight's perspective, Douglass depended upon God
to right the wrongs of human history. Liberation for the
oppressed is eventually in God's hands, and he will one day
intervene on their behalf. God will force his will on people and
nations. Wherever there is suffering and oppression, be it in
the United States or the third-world countries, a retributive
God will eventually eliminate oppression because of his
functional control over the affairs and destiny of human beings.

This study takes issue with Blight's analysis. Though
Blight does mention a shift in Douglass's political thought, he
fails to see a shift in Douglass's theological thought. The
danger of Blight's argument is that he puts Douglass in the
"transcendental temptation" category, "the source of the true
believer's exclamation: 'Only God can save us.'"[11] The
consequence of such a belief is highly "compensatory," which
leads the oppressed to take a passive attitude toward their
condition because God will eventually force his will on human
nature.

In addition, Blight says that "Douglass' God was the God
of black Christianity: benevolent and loving, but also a
deliverer with a special concern for the oppressed. In general

---

[10] David W. Blight, *Frederick Douglass' Civil War: Keeping Faith in Jubliee*
(Baton Rouge: Louisiana State University Press, 1989) 8.

[11] Paul Kurtz, *Toward a New Enlightenment* (New Brunswick: Transaction
Publishers, 1994) 260.

religious outlook, Douglass was a nineteenth-century millennialist."[12] Blight's treatment of Douglass here is inaccurate. Douglass's God was not the God of black Christianity. In fact, Douglass moved away from the beliefs and concepts that many of his fellow slaves held because these beliefs made slaves more likely to acquiesce in their condition.

Furthermore, Douglass was not a millenarian who believed in the "expectation of God's extraordinary intervention in history to destroy an evil age and replace it with a new, eternal creation."[13] The author agrees that Douglass did share in the belief that destruction of slavery would usher in a new era of peace and freedom, but Douglass did not depend upon God to bring liberation to the oppressed. Instead, he elevated the ultimacy of human power to break the chains of bondage. In fact, Douglass blamed the clergy for promoting the idea that God would liberate the oppressed:

> The clergy are to blame for the apathy of the colored people to their own cause. The text, "seek ye first the kingdom of heaven, and its righteousness," has been grossly perverted by the ignorant colored clergy, so that the people wait for God to help them. It is a ridiculous and absurd notion to expect God to deliver us from bondage. We must elevate ourselves by our own efforts.[14]

Here, Douglass acknowledges that there is no power in this world that can be relied upon other than humans themselves.

As far as Douglass was concerned, God was not going to do for humans what they would not do for themselves, and he

---

[12] Blight, *Frederick Douglass' Civil War*, 8.
[13] Ibid., 103.
[14] John W. Blassingame, *The Frederick Douglass Papers*, vol. 2, 1847-54, (New Haven and London: Yale University Press, 1979-85), 170.

endeavored to instill this in the minds of the oppressed. This analysis of Douglass totally impeaches Blight's assertion that "Douglass' God was the God of black Christianity." Douglass had liberated himself from certain beliefs about God in black Christianity that he deemed superstitious. With the exception of Blight, Douglass scholars have agreed about the position from which Douglass moved, but there is still disagreement as to where Douglass ended up in his beliefs.

Waldo E. Martin, for instance, argues that Douglass abandoned traditional forms of Christian theism in favor of Christian liberalism because the nineteenth-century expression of Christian conservatism, with its strong belief in divine determinism in human affairs, was replaced with a theological posture that substantially elevates the human agent in human affairs and history. Humans are no longer considered as Calvin viewed them, depraved or as a "lump of perdition," but as living qualities of great potential that can change or modify the society in which they live. Through their own ingenuity, humans can create a just society without postulating a God who will do it for them. Douglass believed that only by the efforts of humans can there be social progress because divine power alone has never totally wiped out evil. From Martin's perspective, Douglass found it blasphemous to credit God for humans' deeds; therefore, he took the responsibility of human affairs and destiny from God's shoulders and placed it squarely in human hands:

> Progressive social change, Douglass surmised, depended more clearly upon the efforts of man himself than upon those of an unseen and inscrutable God operating ambiguously and indirectly in human affairs through human conduct…. God's will and actions could only be realized, he believed, through human intermediaries. He rejected the immobilizing idea of

waiting for God to end slavery "in the fullness of time"...[arguing that] emancipation could not be left to chance or miracle.[15]

Martin's analysis of Douglass's replacing God's overruling sovereignty for the ontological status of humans in human affairs is entirely correct. Yet Martin attributes Douglass's change from a traditional God-centered religion to a liberal human religion to several factors other than the one this study is asserting, namely a liberation theology. Martin says that "the trenchant Garrisonian criticism of the American church and clergy for their ties to slavery...his belief in the notion of human perfectibility rooted in an evangelical religion stressing 'good works' over the fine points of faith and metaphysics...also found the liberal and ethical emphasis of Theodore Parker's Transcendental Unitarianism...in combination with his thoroughgoing adherence to Enlightenment principles of natural law and rationality"[16] transformed Douglass to religious liberalism.

This study agrees that Douglass was influenced a great deal by these ideologies, but to conclude that these influences were the "die cast" for Douglass's shift to liberalism is an inaccurate description of his transformation. Douglass's shift to liberalism was due to his developing a theological perspective that was conducive to liberation. Long before Douglass was influenced by Garrisonian orthodoxy, transcendental Unitarianism, and enlightenment principles of natural law and rationality, he was already developing a liberation theology. Some of the influences Martin mentioned did have an impact for social reform, and Douglass incorporated them into his theological perspective. But what did not fit into Douglass's

---

[15] Waldo E. Martin, *The Mind of Frederick Douglass* (Chapel Hill: University of North Carolina Press, 1984) 176.

[16] Ibid., 178.

liberation theology, he discarded, as he did with Christian conservatism and Garrisonian orthodoxy.

Garrisonism could be described as liberal because it went against Christian conservatism at that time. However, this does not necessarily mean it was liberating. Douglass disagreed with the Garrisonians at several points. Whatever was discovered to be a hindrance to liberation, Douglass discarded, as a liberation thinker should do to avoid any obstruction to liberation. Therefore, the influences that Martin mentioned to be the die cast for Douglass's transformation, this study attributes to Douglass's development of a liberation theology and considers this a better description for his transformation.

On the basis of the foregoing analysis, there exists a second unsettled issue among scholars that addresses the cause of Douglass's evolutionary shift in theology. William Van Deburg traces the cause of Douglass's theological shift to psychological factors, rather than an impetus for economic, social, and political reform:

> Scorned by white churchmen both as a black Christian and as a Garrisonian abolitionist, Douglass found it impossible to respect the religious profession of Christians whose characters were tarnished by anti-Negro prejudice. Eventually this feeling contributed importantly to his rejection of the "wonder-working power" of the Christian God.... The rejection experience closed off certain avenues of belief and opened up others which never have been seriously considered had the rejection experience not occurred.[17]

---

[17] William Lloyd Van Deburg, "Rejected of Men: The Changing Religious Views of William Lloyd Garrison and Frederick Douglass," Ph.D. diss., Michigan State University, 1973, 340.

Van Deburg assertings that Douglass moved to the other side of the theological spectrum because his ego had been bruised; he felt slighted, demeaned, and rejected. To counteract this feeling of unmeaningfulness and despair, Douglass shifted his theological position to satisfy psychological needs. Van Deburg's argument has ranked psychology above liberation. He has reduced Douglass's theological position to a search for comfort, to a coping mechanism that intervened as Douglass struggled with apparently hopeless situations. However, the logical outcome of this argument would be quietism, a refusal to correct the present situation.

This study's perspective challenges Van Deburg's position because it is not tenable. Douglass was not seeking psychological solace because of a bruised ego, for he could have easily found such solace in the belief system of the black church. Howard Thurman gives a description of someone who is in need of psychological healing:

> A man may be buffeted about by his environment, or may be regarded as a nobody in the general community; a woman may be a nurse in a white family in which the three-year-old child in her care calls her by her first name, thus showing quite unconsciously the contempt in which she is held by his parents. When this Negro man and this Negro woman come to their church, however, for one terribly fulfilling moment they are somebody.[18]

Thurman points out how the psychological needs of the oppressed find nurturing in the church, but no encouragement to change the oppressive structures that constantly bruise the

---

[18] Howard Thurman, *The Luminous Darkness* (New York: Harper & Row, 1965) 21.

selfhood. To meet psychological needs and leave the economic, social, and political needs unmet plays to the advantage of the oppressor—precisely what the oppressed have been doing for centuries—and is the reason the activities of the black church have been unsuccessful in bringing about true reform instead of mere tokenism.

This study concurs that the psychological needs of Douglass were very important, but they certainly were not the causal thrust for his shift to the other side of the theological spectrum. Douglass was developing a theological apparatus that would effectively exterminate economic, social, and political oppression, and this development went far beyond the requirement of satisfying his psychological needs. Douglass's shift was not psychological, but the fit between a theological belief and its usefulness for social reform.

Another scholar, John Turner Grayson, gives another cause for Douglass's evolutionary shift in theology. He purports that Douglass was greatly influenced by Western enlightenment principles of natural law and rationality. Douglass's views of God, man, and reason were the critical variables for his transformation:

> Philosophically, the concepts of God, Man, and Reason are revealed as central in the transformation of Douglass' religious beliefs from theism to a modified humanism.... But it was his humanism which finally broke the mystical and "other worldly" spell religious ideas had upon him, thus clearing the way for the social theories of liberation which dominated his later thought.[19]

---

[19] John T. Grayson, "Frederick Douglass Intellectual Development: His Concept of God, Man, and Nature in Light of American and European Influences," Ph.D. diss., Columbia University, 1981, 2.

Grayson's description indeed affirms that Douglass moved toward a liberation theology, and this study is in agreement with him. But whereas Grayson traces Douglass's shift toward "modified humanism" to Western enlightenment principles of natural law and rationality, this study declares that Douglass was motivated by the demand for a liberation theology that called for an end to economic, social, and political oppression. It is the vision of liberation theology—that is, the specific set of beliefs and values that counter oppression—that best explains the movement of Douglass's thought.

Also, this study challenges Grayson's classification of the social theories of liberation. Whereas Grayson argues that there is a movement from traditional Christian theism to a "modified humanism," this study claims that the movement was not from traditional Christian theism to humanism but from traditional Christian theism to another form of theism, the form of theism that is required by a liberation theologian. Grayson has not considered these more recent forms of theism; he only deals with one understanding of theism, "theocentric theism." But liberation theology's more recent form of theism, "humanocentric theism," illuminates a quite different understanding of theism.

Humanocentric theism asserts that humans are responsible for bringing about change in the human situation. It is the will of God to protest against unjust structures that cause others to suffer. This new variety of theism does not undermine God's sovereignty; it only affirms human freedom, which God has delegated to human beings. William R. Jones says, "The essential feature of [humanocentric theism] is the advocacy of the functional ultimacy of [humans]. [Humans] must act as if [they] were the ultimate valuator or the ultimate agent in human history or both. Thus God's responsibility for the crimes and errors of human history is reduced if not effectively eliminated."[20] Douglass said, "I had now penetrated to the secret of all slavery and of all oppression, and had ascertained their true foundation to be in the pride, the power and the avarice of man."[21] Furthermore, "what man can make, man can unmake."[22] This is a clear example of Douglass's humano-centric theism. He did not blame God for the crime of slavery and oppression; he blamed humans.

But with the freedom that God has given humans, it is up to humans to block the avarice of other humans who create and produce mischief into law. In short, humanocentric theism is when we are God's hands and feet in the struggle for justice. Humanocentric theism is a more accurate description of how Douglass moved to than Grayson's "modified humanism."

In conclusion, this has been an honest attempt to motivate Douglass scholars to reconsider their respective positions concerning Douglass's theological and philosophical development. In arguing the case, this study attempts to open up the terms of the scholars' dispute, and to see Douglass as a liberation thinker who anticipated a liberation theology. The evolution of a liberation theology has shed much light on the subject of Douglass's philosophical and theological development, and it is the author's hope that this new analysis has brought us closer to understanding this great advocate of human freedom.

---

[20] Jones, *Is God A White Racist?*, xxii.

[21] Frederick Douglass, *The Life and Times of Frederick Douglass* (New York: Pathway Press, 1941) 96.

[22] Frederick Douglass, *My Bondage and My Freedom* (New York: Arno Press, 1969) 90.

CONCLUSION

There is no question that Douglass is a shining symbol of liberation and an excellent example of a self-made man. His legacy cannot be undervalued. He stands as one of the most authoritative voices in commanding and demanding the total liberation of the oppressed. Black and feminist protest in America since Douglass is indebted to him for being a trailblazer in helping others to cross over the bridge to a fuller humanity. Benjamin Quarles stated, "In a three-fold sense Douglass was a bridge-builder-a bridge between slavery and freedom, between Negroes and whites, between struggle and success."[1] Douglass is the quintessential example of dedication, hard work, aggressiveness, and perseverance. His life is an archetype of what others could become. James McCune Smith put it this way:

> When a man raises himself from the lowest condition in society to the highest, mankind pays him the tribute of their admiration; when he accomplishes this elevation by native energy, guided by prudence and wisdom, their admiration is increased; but when his

---

[1] Benjamin Quarles, ed., *Frederick Douglass* (Washington, D.C.: Associated Publishers, Inc., 1948) 177.

course, onward and upward...furthermore proves a possible, what hitherto been regarded as an impossible, reform, then he becomes a burning and a shining light, on which the aged may look with gladness, the young with hope, and the down-trodden, as a representative of what they may themselves become.[2]

Although Douglass's life is an American success story, his religious persuasion rendered him less popular in the eyes of black and white conservatives. Douglass's views on religion put him outside the circle of Christian orthodoxy. Douglass was very suspicious of religion at an early age, especially after he witnessed his master's conversion, which turned out to be a farce. He witnessed the whipping of slaves while Bible Scriptures were quoted to justify the cruel treatment. The gross misrepresentation of the Bible and the sanction of the church during slavery set Douglass at odds with American Christianity, and for this reason he was opposed to giving Bibles to the slaves before they were given their freedom. Some thought that Douglass himself was irreligious for advising those who were concerned about the religious nature of the slaves that it was "infinitely better to send them a pocket compass and a pistol."[3]

Douglass was more concerned about the liberty of the slaves than about their religious well-being. He could not trust religion to get him or his people out of slavery, given the way religion was used to justify slavery. Douglass came to rely upon human action to bring about social and political reform. He tried the traditional way of praying to God for deliverance, but his prayers yielded no results without him taking action to do

---

[2] James McCune Smith, "Introduction," *My Bondage and My Freedom* (1855 reprint; New York: Dover, 1969) xvii.
[3] Benjamin Quarles, "Introduction," *Narrative of the Life of Frederick Douglass* (Cambridge: Harvard University Press, 1960) ix.

something for himself. Donald B. Gibson stated that Douglass "becomes one of our early pragmatists (qualifiedly so) in that he comes to believe in a very practical Christianity, a world view that places politics ahead of religion insofar as the managing of the affairs of life is concerned."[4] Douglass's experience in life proved that prayer alone is ineffective, for "he had offered many prayers for freedom, but he did not get it until he prayed with his legs."[5] Douglass encouraged his oppressed brothers and sisters to be self-reliant rather than trust an intrusion of help from the outside: "The man who lies down a fool at night, hoping that he will awake wise in the morning, will rise up in the morning as he laid down in the evening."[6]

The central problem Douglass detected among the oppressed was their miseducation/misreligion, which Carter G. Woodson, Benjamin Mays, and others expounded upon years later. Though Douglass did not deny the existence of God, he could get a glimpse of God through the actions of human beings. The presence of God was not seen exclusively in the affairs of humanity. The oppressed believed too much in the exclusive presence of God in human affairs, which Douglass saw yielded no results. Douglass was simply saying to the oppressed, "Faith without work is dead." In one of his most popular lectures, "Self-Made Men," which he presented in many places, Douglass emphasized human activity, not divine, in human affairs. The execution of human wills is what makes human beings in the world, not God, fate, or destiny. Douglass further stated, "So far as the laws of the universe have been

---

[4] Donald B. Gibson, "Faith, Doubt, and Apostasy: Evidence of Things in Frederick Douglass' Narrative," in *Frederick Douglass: New Literary and Historical Essays* (New York: Cambridge University Press, 1990) 91.

[5] Frederick May Holland, Frederick Douglass: The Colored Orator (New York: Funk & Wagnalls Co., Inc. 1981) 67.

[6] Holland's discussion of Douglass's speech, "Self-Made Men," 258.

discovered and understood, they seem to teach that the mission of man's improvement and perfection has been wholly committed to man himself. He is to be his own savior or his own destroyer. He has neither angels to help him, nor devils to hinder him."[7]

As stated earlier, Douglass did value religion only if it was used to correction oppression. In America he found religion an arch supporter of oppression, which he protested against, along with the indoctrination of this kind of religion in his people. He desperately wanted his people to be delivered from the beliefs and values that kept them docile and wishing for relief in heaven when they could have it on earth. What Douglass discovered about religion, Peter Berger wrote about years later:

> Religion legitimates social institutions by bestowing upon them an ultimately valid ontological status, that is, by locating them within a sacred and cosmic frame of reference.... Let the institutional order be so interpreted as to hide, as much as possible, its constructed [human] character.... Let the people forget that this order was established by men and continues to be dependent upon the consent of men. Let them believe that, in acting out the institutional programs that have been imposed upon them, they are but realizing the deepest aspirations of their own being and putting themselves in harmony with the fundamental order of the universe.[8]

Douglass wanted the oppressed to see the human hand behind religion and that oppression is not a divine construction, but a human one. He wanted them to oppose oppression and any religion that justified it. Until the

---

[7] 29 October 1890, recorded in Holland, *Frederick Douglass*, 336.

[8] Peter Berger, *The Sacred Canopy* (New York: Doubleday, 1969) 33.

oppressed dumped the religion of their oppressors, there could be no progress. Douglass stated his hope for the future of his people:

My hope for the future of my race is further supported by the rapid decline of an emotional, shouting, and thoughtless religion. Scarcely in any direction can there be found a less favorable field for mind or morals than where such a religion prevails. It abounds in the wildest hopes and fears, and in blind unreasoning faith. Instead of adding to faith virtue, its tendency is to substitute faith for virtue, and is a deadly enemy to our progress.[9]

Given how religion has been used as a tool to oppress others, no one can blame Douglass for his mistrust of it. What we do know is that many of the themes found in liberation theology are also found in the thinking of Frederick Douglass. As Douglass tried to rescue his people from misreligion, liberation theology is trying to rescue Christianity from the exegetical hermeneutical interpretation of oppressors. Douglass's life and thought represent what it means to struggle against oppression and the religion that holds it in place. This is why we see his life as a precursor to liberation theology.

---

[9] Frederick Douglass, The Life and Times of Frederick Douglass, (New York: Pathway Press, 1941) 508.

BIBLIOGRAPHY

BOOKS

Akbar, Naim. *Chains and Images of Psychological Slavery*. Tallahassee Florida: Mind Productions & Associates, 1998.

Allen, Norm R. Jr., ed. *African-American Humanism: An Anthology*. New York: Prometheus Books, 1991.

Andrews, William L. *The Oxford Frederick Douglass Reader*. New York: Oxford University Press, 1996.

Aptheker, Herbert. *The Negro People in the United States*. New York: Citadel Press, 1951.

Barbour, Floyd B., ed. *The Black Revolt*. Boston: Porter Sergent Publisher, 1968.

Bedell, George C. *Religion in America*. New York: Macmillan Publishing Co., Inc., 1982.

Bennett, John C. *The Radical Imperative*. Philadelphia: Westminster Press, 1975.

Bennett, Lerone Jr. *Before the Mayflower: A History of the Negro in America*. Baltimore: Penguin Books, 1962.

———. *The Challenge of Blackness*. Chicago: Johnson Publishing Company, 1972.

Berger, Peter. *The Sacred Canopy*. New York: Doubleday, 1969.

Berkovits, Eliezer. *Faith After the Holocaust*. New York: KTAV Publishing House, 1973.

Blassingame, John W. *The Slave Community*. New York: Oxford University Press, 1972.

————. *The Frederick Douglass Papers*. Vols. 1–3. New Haven and London: Yale University Press, 1979–1985.

Blight, David W. *Frederick Douglass' Civil War: Keeping Faith in Jubilee*. Baton Rouge: Louisiana State University Press, 1989.

Boff, Leonardo and Clodovis. *Introducing Liberation Theology*. Maryknoll NY: Orbis Books, 1988.

Bonino, Jose M. *Doing Theology in a Revolutionary Setting*. Philadelphia: Fortress Press, 1975.

Bontemps, Arna. *Free at Last: The Life of Frederick Douglass*. New York: Dodd, Mead & Co., 1971.

Brietman, George, ed. *Malcolm X Speaks*. New York: Grove Press, 1966.

Brown, Robert McAfee. *Gustavo Gutierrez: An Introduction to Liberation Theology*. Maryknoll NY: Orbis Books, 1990.

————. *Makers of Contemporary Theology*. Atlanta: John Knox Press, 1980.

————. *Is Faith Obsolete?* Philadelphia: Westminster Press, 1974.

Brunner, Emil. *The Christian Doctrine of Creation and Redemption*. Philadelphia: Westminster Press, 1952.

Buber, Martin. *Haisdism*. New York: Philosophical Library, 1948.

Cleage, Albert B., *Black Christian Nationalism*. New York: William Morrow and Co., 1972.

Collins, Sheila. *A Different Heaven and Earth*. Valley Forge PA: Judson Press, 1974.

Cone, James H. *God of the Oppressed*. Minnesota: Seabury Press, 1975.

————. *A Black Theology of Liberation*. Maryknoll NY: Orbis Books, 1986. 1970 by J.B. Lippincott Company

————. *Black Theology and Black Power*. Maryknoll NY: Orbis Books, 1997.

————. *The Spirituals and the Blues*. New York: Seabury Press, 1972.

Douglass, Frederick. *The Life and Times of Frederick Douglass*. New York: Pathway Press, 1941.

————. *My Bondage and My Freedom*. New York:Arno Press, 1969.

————. *Narrative of the Life of Frederick Douglass, an American Slave*. New York: Penguin Books, 1982.

DuBois, W. E. B. *The Souls of Black Folk*. Chicago: A. C. McClurg & Co., 1929.

Dunbar, Paul Lawrence. *Lyrics of Lowly Life*. New York: Dodd, Mead and Company, 1897.

Dussel, Enrique. *History and the Theology of Liberation*. A Latin American Perspective, Translated by John Drury. Maryknoll NY: Orbis Books, 1976.

Ellison, Ralph. *Invisible Man*. New York: Random House Publisher, 1947.

Epps, Archie, ed. *The Speeches of Malcolm X at Harvard*. New York: Morrow Press, 1968.

Foner, Philip S., ed. *The Life and Writings of Frederick Douglass*. Vols. 1–5. New York: International Publishers, 1950–1975.

Frazier, E. Franklin. *The Negro Church in America*. New York: Schocken Book, 1974.

————. *Black Bourgeoisie*. New York: Collier Books, 1965.

Freire, Paulo. *Pedagogy of the Oppressed*. New York: Continuum Publishing Company, 1993.

Goizueta, Roberto S. *Liberation, Method And Dialogue*. Atlanta, Georgia: Scholars Press, 1988.

Graham, Shiley. *There Was Once a River: The Heroic Story of Frederick Douglass*. New York: 1947.

Gregory, James M. *Frederick Douglass: The Orator*. New York: Seabury Press, 1975.

Gutierrez, Gustavo. *A Theology of Liberation*. Maryknoll NY: Orbis Books, 1973.

————. *The Truth Shall Make You Free*. Translated by Matthew J. O'Connell. Maryknoll NY: Orbis Books, 1990.

Haselden, Kyle. *The Racial Problem in Christian Perspective*. New York: Harper & Row, 1959.

Herzog, Frederick. *Liberation Theology: Liberation in Light of the Fourth Gospel*. New York: Seabury Press, 1972.

Holland, Frederick May. *Frederick Douglass: The Colored Orator*. New York: Funk & Wagnalls Co., Inc., 1891.

Howard-Pitney, David. *The Afro-American Jeremiad*. Philadelphia: Temple University Press, 1990.

Huggins, Nathan. Irvin *Slave and Citizen: The Life of Frederick Douglass*. Boston: Little Brown & Company, 1980.

Hyman, Harold M. and Leonard W., eds. *Freedom and Reform*. New York: Harper & Row, 1967.

James, Gene G. *The Search for Faith and Justice in the Twentieth Century*. New York: Paragon House Publishers, 1987.

Jones, William R. *Is God A White Racist?* New York: Double Day Anchor, 1973.

Kurtz, Paul. *Toward a New Enlightenment*. New Brunswick Canada: Transaction Publishers, 1994.

Latourette, Kenneth Scott. *A History of Christianity*. New York: Harper & Brothers Publishers, 1953.

Martin, Waldo E. *The Mind of Frederick Douglass*. Chapel Hill: University of North Carolina Press, 1984.

Mays, Benjamin E. *The Negro's God*. New York: Atheneum, 1969.

McClain, William B. *Black People in the Methodist Church*. Nashville: Abingdon Press, 1984.

McFeely, William S. *Frederick Douglass*. New York: W. W. Norton & Company, 1991.

Meier, August. *Negro Thought in America: 1880–1915*. Ann Arbor: University of Michigan Press, 1973.

Niebuhr, Reinhold. *Moral Man and Immoral Society*. New York: Charles Scribner's Sons, 1932.

Nunez C., Emilio. *Liberation Theology*. Translated by Paul E. Sywulka. Chicago: Moody Press, 1985.

O'Brien, John A. *Truths Men Live By*. New York: The Macmillan Publishing Company, 1946.

Paris, Peter J. *The Social Teachings of the Black Church*. Philadelphia: Fortress Press, 1985.

Pinn, Anthony B. *Why, Lord? Suffering and Evil in Black Theology*. New York: The Continuum Publishing Company, 1995.

Quarles, Benjamin, ed.. *Frederick Douglass*. Washington, D.C.: Associated Publishers, Inc., 1948.

Raboteau, Albert J. *Slave Religion*. New York: Oxford University Press, 1978.

Rothenberg, Paula. *Racism and Sexism: An Integrated Study*. New York: St. Martin's Press, 1988.

Sernett, Milton C. *Afro-American Religious History: A Documentary Witness*. Durham: Duke University Press, 1985.

Suchocki, Marjorie Hewitt. *Process Eschatology in Historical Context: The End of Evil*. New York: State University of New York Press, 1988.

Thurman, Howard. *The Luminous Darkness*. New York: Harper & Row, 1965.

———. *Deep River and the Negro Spiritual Speaks of Life and Death*. Richmond, Indiana: Friends United Press, 1975.

Troeltsch, Ernst. *The Social Teaching of the Christian Churches*. Vol. 2. Translated by Olive Wyon. Louisville: Westminster/John Knox Press, 1992.

Wentzel, Fred D. *Epistle to White Christians*. Philadelphia: The Christian Education Press, 1948.

West, Cornel. *Prophesy Deliverance: An Afro-American Revolutionary.* Philadelphia: The Westminster Press, 1982.

Whitehead, Alfred North. *Science and the Modern World.* New York: The Macmillan Company, 1931.

Williams, George Huntston. *The Radical Reformation.* Philadelphia: Westminster Press, 1972.

Wilmore, Gayraud S. *Black Religion and Black Radicalism,* 2nd ed.. Maryknoll NY: Orbis Books, 1983.

Wilmore, Gayraud S., and James H. Cone. *Black Theology: A Documentary History, 1966–1979.* Maryknoll NY: Orbis Books, 1979.

Woodson, Carter G. *Miseducation of the Negro.* Washington, D.C.: Associated Publishers, Inc., 1933, 1969.

———. *Negro Orators and Their Orations.* Washington, D.C.: Associated Publishers, Inc., 1925.

ARTICLES, DISSERTATIONS, AND ESSAYS

Carson, Sharon. "Shaking the Foundation: Liberation Theology in *Narrative of the Life of Frederick Douglass.*" *Religious Lit* 24 (Summer 1992): 19–34.

Cobb, William Daniel. "Morality in the Making: A Look at Some Old Foundations." January 1st – 8th *Century* (January 1975).

DuBois, W. E. B. "A Litany at Atlanta." In *Black Voices,* edited by Abraham Chapman. New York: New American Library, 1968.

Gilkey, Langdon. "Cosmology, Ontology, and the Travail of Biblical Language." *Journal of Religion* 41 (1961).

Grayson, John T. "Frederick Douglass' Intellectual Development: His Concept of God, Man, and Nature in Light of American and European Influences." Ph.D. dissertation, Columbia University, 1981.

Hunt, James B. "The Faith Journey of Frederick Douglass, 1818–1895." *Christian Scholar's Review* 15/3 (1986): 228–46.

Jones, William R. "Is Faith in God Necessary for the Just Society? Insights from Liberation Theology." In *The Search for Faith and Justice in the Twentieth Century,* edited by Gene G. James. New York: Paragon Press, 1987.

———. "Purpose and Method in Liberation Theology: Implications for an Interim Assessment." In *Liberation Theology: North American Style,* edited by Deane William Ferm. New York: Vertizon, 1987.

———. "The Religious Legitimation of Counter-violence: Insights from Latin American Liberation Theology." In *The Terrible Meek: Revolution and Religion in Cross-cultural Perspective*, edited by Lonnie D. Kliver. New York: Paragon Press, 1987.

———. "Process Theology: Guardian of the Oppressor or Goad to the Oppressed: An Interim Assessment." *Process Studies* 18/4 (Winter 1989).

———. "Theological Response to 'The Church and Urban Policy.'" *Journal of the Society for Common Insights* 2 (1978): 49–57.

———. *Commemoration*. Florida Endowment for the Humanities. Edited by E. C. Riley, Ann Henderson, and George Schurr, 1987.

Long, Charles. "The Black Reality: Toward a Theology of Freedom." *Criterion* (Spring–Summer 1969): 2–7.

Roberts, J. Deotis. "Black Liberation Theism." *Journal of Religious Thought* 33 (Spring–Summer 1976): 25–35.

Van Deburg, William Lloyd. "Rejected of Men: The Changing Religious Views of William Lloyd Garrison and Frederick Douglass." Ph.D. dissertation, Michigan State University, 1974.

———. "Frederick Douglass: Maryland Slave to Religious Liberal." *Maryland Historical Magazine* 69 (Spring 1974): 27–43.

JOURNALS

Anti-Slavery Bugle (Salem, Ohio), 1860

The Colgate Rochester Divinity School Bulletin (Rochester, New York), 1939–1940.

North Star (Rochester, New York), 1847–1851

INDEX